BRAZIL

Times Editions · Les Editions du Pacifique
422 Thomson Road, Singapore 1129.
© Copyright by Times Editions
1978, 1981, 1983, 1984, 1986.
Printed in Singapore by Tien Wah Press.
All rights reserved for all countries.
Distributed by Distribuidora Record
de Serviços de Imprensa S.A.
Rua Argentina, 171-CEP 20921
Caixa Postal 884, Rio de Janeiro, RJ.
ISBN: 9971-40-089-8

BRAZIL

CARLOS DE SÁ MOREIRA

LES·EDITIONS·DU·PACIFIQUE

DISTRIBUIDORA RECORD

contents

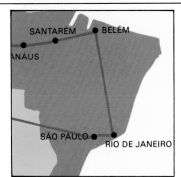

INTRODUCTION

Like James Thurber's Walter Mitty, who was always dreaming of escaping from his wife to distant adventures, all of us living in mass consumer societies dream of escaping and discovering adventure in exotic lands. A few names conjure up the magic and excitement of such adventure: names such as Tahiti, Bali, Thailand and Brazil.

Air travel now puts these once inaccessible places within our reach. Previously, the high fares limited such trips to a few fortunate people, but in the last few years cheaper fares and charter flights have led to increased travel all over the world.

Brazil, holds a special fascination for everyone partly because it sounds exotic, partly because of its vast size, diversity and tropical climate, but also because of its future as a great world power in the 21st century. Only a few Americans know anything about this power-to-be and such rare knowledge centers on coffee and its history, the new capital: Brasilia, the bay of Rio de Janeiro and its beaches with those perenially beautiful girls, soccer and its king Pelé, the Carnival of Rio, the samba, the Amazon jungle through which a highway a couple of thousand miles long is relentlessly penetrating, and the industries which have created a Brazilian economic miracle. This undoubtedly provides us with a good idea of a certain aspect of Brazil but leaves us with an incomplete picture of the country as a whole.

Brazil is a huge and varied country, bigger than Western Europe, almost half the size of the United States and accounting for nearly half of South America's land mass and population. A fascinating adventure awaits tourists visiting this immense land, most of whose territory is situated in the zone between the Equator and the Tropic of Capricorn. Brazil's landscapes range from white, sandy beaches curving along the blue ocean on the eastern coast of the country to the parched and scorched sertao in the north, and the lush, green forests of the Amazon, and distant foothills of the Andes mountains.

Although this book has not tried to present a total picture, it will show some of the other aspects of Brazil and describe Brazil's major tourist attractions. If you are planning a trip to Brazil and have little idea of what to expect, such information should help you to enjoy a distant adventure as well as discover an exotic land.

This book is not a geographical description, a sociological study or an economic summary, nor is it a complete guide. It is simply a succession of ideas, suggestions and useful information. Most travellers have difficulty in choosing places in which to stop, a necessary step if planning a trip, owing to the immense size of the country and the limited amount of time available to most tourists.

Brazil is the fifth country in the world for size after the Soviet Union, Canada, China and the United States. Its 2,286,473 sq. miles represent an area the surface of which is 12 times that of Texas. To go from Belem in the north to Porto Alegre in the south via Brasilia, you travel a distance longer than that between New York and San Francisco.

A traveller with a great deal of time can spend months making an exciting and incomparably varied tour of Brazil but if you have only one, two, three or a

maximum of four weeks at your disposal, you should plan to stop in a few important places.

In order to underline this, we have divided the book into six chapters, each of which contains information on a single region as well as information on a large number of important places to visit.

One chapter describes a single city, Salvador de Bahia; another covers Belo Horizonte (capital of Minas Gerais) and some of the excursions which you can make from it; and three chapters deal with vast regions: the South, the Northeast and Amazonia with three or four interesting places described in each chapter.

In addition, in the chapter on Rio de Janeiro readers will find information on Brasilia despite the distance between these two cities. It is easy to visit both owing to daily air shuttle services. Many tourists and busy businessmen going only to Rio consider a trip to the new capital a must.

For each stop, a number of places to visit has been suggested (city, beach, church, monument, museum or walking tour) not only because of their intrinsic value but also because of their importance as tourist sites, the easiness with which they can be reached and proximity to hotels and highways. Airlines and organized excursions are also listed.

Such a choice is necessarily subjective. The important thing about a trip is not the number of things you see but rather the impression they make on you. Everyone likes to talk about his or her personal feelings about a site, give a number of tips and discuss experiences with potential travellers.

If the rocks sculpted by the wind at Vila Velha struck you as exceptional during a trip to Brazil, if you experience sensational fishing off the island of Bananal, if you were charmed by old towns such as Prarti or if you made some memorable excursions into the wild stretches of Mato Grosso, you may be surprised not to find them listed here. Many tourist sites deserve a stop in Brazil, but you will have to choose from among the multitude of things to see.

We shall suggest a number of tours in the chapter on ``Useful Information'' in order to help you plan your trip.

An American tourist generally flies to Brazil and, once there, uses planes as the easiest means of transportation owing to the distances involved in travelling around this vast country. We have suggested itineraries which take maximum advantage of the current system of air fares. American tourists can discover much of Brazil in this way without spending much more than the cost of a simple round-trip ticket.

Some travellers wish to visit other South American countries on a trip to Brazil, for instance Peru and Argentina. We have provided some data on this so that a trip can be planned with a maximum of stops in various countries under interesting conditions.

A complete visit to Brazil should include stops in the places mentioned in the six chapters of this work. The traveller in a hurry will profit from limiting himself to a few stops and spending enough time in each stop rather than rushing from place to place in an attempt to cover everything. Going to Brazil is no longer an adventure as it only takes a few hours to go from New York to Rio de Janeiro. You can easily return sometime in the future!

RIO/BRASÍLIA

Rio de Janeiro, justly, is often referred to as the ''marvelous city''. No tourist in the world who has already seen pictures of it in movies, books and magazines or on TV escapes a feeling of rapture once there. Rio is a unique symphony of sea and city, beach and mountain over which hovers the contagious joy of a samba or a song.

The navigator André Gonçalves, leading an expedition to explore the coast of Brazil, discovered the Bay of Guanabara on 1 January 1502. In remembrance of that date and convinced that he had found the estuary of a long river, he called the site Rio de Janeiro, the River of January. A town was founded 60 years later by Estacio de Sa, whose father the Governor General of Brazil, ordered him to rid the region of French Huguenots trying to colonize the area around the bay.

Two centuries later gold was found in the region of Minas Gerais. The economic center of the country then naturally moved south and in 1763 Rio de Janeiro became the capital of Brazil. Since then, the city has never stopped growing. It has grown to such an extent that it continues to play a predominant role in all sectors of Brazilian life despite the inauguration of Brasilia as the new capital in 1960.

The tourist visiting Rio — like the inhabitant of Rio who works there all week — dreams of the beach. Rio's beaches curve for more than 120 miles and offer unlimited possibilities. No other large metropolis in the world can offer its inhabitants or visitors such a close stretch of sand and ocean. You need only cross the street and there it is. The beaches stretch out, one after another. You can go swimming in the winter as well as in the summer; you can sleep or exercise, get a tan or play ball; you can swim or enjoy the surf, admire the girls whose proverbial beauty is the subject of many songs, or meet everyone worth knowing in Rio. In short, Rio's beaches are a paradise for whiling away time, a unique space for sports and a meeting place where everyone finds each other.

Along the bay the beaches of Flamengo, Botafogo and Urca are quiet. Facing the ocean, the beaches of Leme, Copacabana, Arpoador, Ipanema and Leblon are battered by high waves. Depending on fashion one or the other is more or less crowded. A fashionable inhabitant of Rio may wish to be seen at Castelhino or at some special point along Ipanema. But the tourist, deriding this snobbish attitude, will indifferently choose one or the other. Whichever he chooses, he will always find the same ocean, the same fine sand and the same wall of skyscrapers etched against the rocky mountains.

The life of the beach does not only take place on the sand. The adjacent sidewalks are filled with bars and restaurants which place their tables in the open, You can sit down at any hour and sip the national drink, ''batida'', made of *cachaça* (sugar cane spirits), lime, sugar and ice.

This is the ideal place to encounter one of the leading tourist attractions of the city, the inhabitants of Rio. Merry, relaxed and humming snatches of songs, the inhabitants of Rio are always ready to meet new friends. These people with the gift of the gab and a soft heart are hard-working, contrary to gossip. The pace of life in Rio is quiet and peaceful except for the fact that there are more cars in the streets than in almost any other city in the world.

This pleasant atmosphere is also found in the center of the city, which differs considerably from the beach area. Copacabana and Ipanema are relatively new districts with modern buildings but the center of Rio preserves the character of an old Portuguese town. Strolling along the streets near the Praça Quinze, you will find beautiful old buildings such as the Viceroy's Palace now the central Post Office. Dominating this section of Rio on the top of a hill, the Monastery of São Bento has the richest church in Rio, entirely covered with gold.

Two other churches deserve a visit not only for their beauty but also for the admirable view of the city which they offer. São Francisco da Penitência (Saint Francis-of-the-Penitence) on top of another hill facing the Largo da Carioca is a baroque jewel. You take an elevator to reach it. In the background is the well-preserved 18th century Carioca Aqueduct with its elegant arches overlooking an ever-changing urban landscape. A little further on, the baroque Church of the Gloria do Outeiro adds a gracious and soft touch to Rio's modern center. From it too, you have a splendid view of the city.

We should also mention the *Largo do Boticario,* the Apothecary's Square, in the Cosme Velho section, a green, poetic oasis which has conserved intact the atmosphere of old Rio.

Contrasting with this still relatively recent past, the city offers a number of futurist images. Modern Brazilian architecture was born in Rio in 1937 with the construction of the Ministry of Education, designed by Oscar Niemeyer. New buildings such as the Petrobrás building, churches such as the new Cathedral, elevated highways, tunnels and gigantic cloverleafs endow the city with a hint of what it will look like in the year 2000.

Two of these transformations have profoundly influenced Rio's general aspect. The Flamengo embankment has been entirely reclaimed from the sea and has gardens landscaped by Burle Marx. Two buildings stand out on this embankment, the Modern Art Museum and the Monument to the Dead of the 2nd World War. New avenues lead to Copacabana but you should take enough time to walk at leisure through the gardens which are always full of cheerful people and to enjoy the view of Sugar Loaf Mountain.

The other transformation to Rio's landscape is the bridge across the bay connecting the metropolis with Niteroi. The bridge is over 8 miles long, has six lanes of traffic, handles 20,000 vehicles a day, and in the center rises to a height of 237 ft. over the water so that ships may pass under it. It is worth driving back and forth over the bridge or seeing it from the water by taking a boat over to Niteroi on the other side of the bay.

The excursion is even more interesting if you go by boat to Paqueta, the quiet, romantic island at one end of the Bay of Guanabara, because you will pass under the bridge. Trips across the bay are also organized on passenger boats, offering tourists a view of the city and the bridge and going around Sugar Loaf as far as Copacabana.

There is one thing you must visit in Rio: the Botanical Gardens, founded by the future King John VI in 1808. Its avenue of royal palm trees, 132 ft. high, may remind you of the nave of a cathedral: the trunks of the trees are as smooth as columns and the branches stretch out toward each other on the top, forming a vault. This area of 345 acres contains more than 5,000 species of trees and thousands of decorative plants. The atmosphere is so peaceful that you will be unaware of time passing.

You should also make two excursions up Corcovado and Sugar Loaf. The first can be done either by car over a steep road through a forest or by a small cog-railway which climbs more than 2,310 ft. in 20 minutes. But it is much more interesting to include this excursion in a more comprehensive tour passing by the Vista Chinese (Chinese View) and the Mesa do Imperator (Emperor's Table) near the Botanical Gardens and then going up the Estrada do Redentor. Along this route you have a number of superb views of Rio before reaching the top of Corcovado.

Once there, you still have 200 steps to climb, but your fatigue will disappear when you reach the top of the steps and arrive at the base of the statue of Christ the Redeemer.

A narrow terrace overlooks a chasm. In front is the cove of Botafogo with Sugar Loaf Mountain; on the left the center of Rio, the bridge, the inner bay, and, in the background, the Organ Mountains; on the right between the mountains and the sea, Copacabana. Beyond are Ipanema, the lagoon, the rock of the Two Brothers and, lost on the horizon, the ocean. It is a unique vista, one of the marvels of the world.

Going up Sugar Loaf is completely different. It begins by offering you the thrill of taking glass cable cars, one for the first part of the ascent as far as Urca Mountain and the other lasting 40 minutes for the lift up to the top of Sugar Loaf. There, at an altitude of 1,320 ft., you will enjoy another equally spectacular view of Rio. If you plan to take photos, remember that the morning is the best time to do so here for Corcovado it is better to take pictures in the afternoon. Both sites offer fabulous views of Rio at twilight when the lights of the city are turned on.

The best time of year to visit Rio is during the Carnival. Although most of the folk festivities in the street have disappeared, the balls and the samba club parade are spectacles unparalleled in the world. The parade is worth the trip.

Ten to twelve clubs, each consisting of two to four thousand members, present a show based on Brazilian history or folklore. Each club has its own samba and colors used in all the club's costumes.

The arrival of a samba club is preceded by a delegation waving to the public. Then come the ranks depicting the different scenes of the scenario in an enchanting succession of costumes. Marvels of imagination and work, some scenes are extremely lavish.

Next appear the *passistas* and the *ritmistas,* virtuosos of the samba and the drum and acrobatics par excellence; followed by the master of ceremonies and a woman bearing the club's colors and waving the flag for all to see. Everyone sings the samba which is taken up by the public until the band formed of a wide range of percussion instruments drowns the voices with its vibrant rhythm.

All of these elements — samba, scenario, band, costumes, passistas, flag bearer — are ranked by a jury whose job is to choose the best club of the year.

The competition between the clubs makes the parade more lavish, more enchanting and more perfect every year; it is, in short, a spectacle which is unique in the world.

Although the clubs only parade with their lavish costumes during the Carnival, you may attend rehearsals in the evening during weekends beginning in August. The most spectacular are those of the Salgueiro, Portela, Mangueira and Imperio Serrano clubs.

Another spectacle which you should not miss is that of a soccer match at the Maracaña stadium. The supporters of the two teams wave their flags, yell with indescribable enthusiasm when the *Flamengo* scores a goal and throw talcum into the air when the *Fluminense* win.

The soccer champion Pelé has become an historical figure and a plaque at the Maracaña stadium commemorates his 1,000th goal, a performance which no other player has ever equalled. Although Pelé no longer plays soccer, other stars have made their name and a good match at Maracaña is a must in Rio, especially if held at night.

In addition, there is much to do at night in Rio. The city has many theaters and movie houses. Amusements range from talking on cafe terraces over countless glasses of *chope* (light beer) to night-clubs where you can hear the best composers and performers of popular Brazilian music. You will also find restaurants catering to all tastes and pocketbooks but with a common bond: high quality fish, shrimps, *churrasco* and *feijoada*.

Among popular places to visit in the State of Rio de Janeiro are Petropolis, 35 miles from Rio and reached over a steep, scenic mountain road; and the popular beaches of Cabo Frio and Agra dos Reis. However, for the traveller anxious to devour continents and organizing a trip in terms of flight hours, one or two free days in Rio provide an opportunity to fulfill the dream of visiting Brasilia.

Flying into Brasilia is quite impressive. After flying over hundreds of miles of still deserted landscapes, passengers suddenly see a forest of buildings rising on the horizon. The sensation is perhaps even more impressive for those arriving by car or bus after driving many hours and then suddenly coming upon this vision of the future.

Brasilia is located on a broad empty plain in the heart of the country's undeveloped Sertão, at an altitude of 3,960 ft., 630 miles from Rio de Janeiro. Not in a region of forests, as is commonly — and incorrectly — thought, Brasilia has been built in the unpopulated uplands of the State of Goías. The city lacked vegetation in its first years. But since, parks have been created and a forest of trees and plants has been planted; and Brasilia is now developing in the middle of trees, flowers and gardens.

The idea of an inland capital was an old national dream. Even before independence, the Minister José Bonifacio strongly recommended the project in order to develop and populate the interior. The Constitution of the Republic in

1891 called for the transfer of the capital. Work, finally begun in 1956 at the insistence of the then new president, Juscelino Kbitschek, was carried out at record speed so that the new capital could be inaugurated in 1960 before the end of his term in office.

The project is a success. Brasilia has continued to grow and today has a population of about five hundred thousand half of which is under the age of 14. And the transfer of foreign embassies has given it the indispensable cosmopolitan element which it lacked.

The city can be visited in a few hours. But to admire the beauty of Brasilia's architecture you should see the city at night when the buildings are illuminated. The sight is enchanting, especially if preceded by a magnificent sunset which can best be seen from the other side of Lake Paranoa, a large, artificial lake created by damming the Paranoa River. The profile of the buildings is etched at that time against a fiery sky in total silence. The vision, which lasts a very short time, is fantastic.

The center of Brasilia is the Praça dos Tres Poderes (Square of the Three Powers), so named because it contains the Congress buildings, the Palacia do Planalto (President's Office) from which the President of Brazil governs the nation, and the Supreme Court building in front of which is an excellent statue of Justice. The latter two buildings, consisting of three floors each, seem to float in space, supported by elegant columns. The impressive, architecturally lyrical Congress buildings, President's Office and Supreme Court building in the Praça dos Tres Poderes were designed by Oscar Niemeyer, the famous Brazilian architect.

The Capitol in the center, consists of two identical 28-storey buildings, the highest in the city, and two low buildings topped by domes, one of which is concave, the Chamber of Deputies, and the other convex, the Senate.

The Eixo Monumental, running east-west from the Praça dos Tres Poderes, is a 5-mile long, 825-ft. wide avenue along which are located the ministry buildings, all of which are identical except for the Ministry of Justice, a magnificent building with artificial cascades between its concrete columns, and the Ministry of Foreign Affairs, the Itamarati, the most beautiful building in Brasilia.

The Itamarati seems to rise from water with its slender marble columns forming arches. When the water is calm, the ministry is reflected as in a mirror; when there is a breeze, the water reflects its movement on the columns and seems to endow the marble with life. This phenomenon can best be seen from the last floor of the ministry with its hanging garden designed by Roberto Burle Marx. This terrace, used for official receptions, leads directly to reception rooms and the banquet hall. The terrace and the hanging garden can be visited in the afternoon with special permission from the ministry.

The Cathedral of Brasilia, also on the Eixo Monumental, and built in the shape of the crown of thorns, can be visited in the day or in the evening when it is illuminated. Sixteen concrete columns 132 ft. high rise skyward; the space between them contains iridescent glass creating a hymn of light and shadow in the immense circular nave. The pattern of light and shadow changes during the day as the sun moves from east to west casting different designs on the floor of the Cathedral.

The Church of Dom Bosco is also beautiful, but in a completely different way. This church is a very interesting building constructed largely of blue glass radiating a deep, yet mysterious, light when struck by the bright sun and a soft, quiet light when the sun's rays are weaker.

A competition for the best general plan for Brasilia was won by the city planner Lucio Costa who laid out the city in the shape of a bent bow and arrow, the bent bow roughly following the shores of a large lake created by damming the Paranoa River. Along the curve of the bow is the residential area to the right of which is the "arrow," the Eixo Monumental. The tip of the arrow corresponds to the Praça dos Tres Poderes.

According to a proverb, "the human body in Brasilia is divided into three parts, head, torso and wheels." Distances in Brasilia are enormous. The city was planned for the automobile and to move around the new capital you will need to use a car or bus. Intersections are avoided by means of underpasses and cloverleafs and there are no traffic jams, except along the W 3 avenue parallel to the Eixo Monumental. This avenue was not part of the original plan but, as shops opened there during the construction of Brasilia, it has become the busiest commercial thoroughfare in the city.

The residential area on the curve of the bow consists of large apartment blocks, the "Super-Quadras." Each unit contains 11 six-storey buildings standing on columns. Each "Super-Quadra" houses 3,000 people and has its own school, garden, playgrounds and sports fields. There is only one exit from these blocks; and a driver entering a Super-Quadra without knowing its plan could drive around for some time without ever finding his way out. This pleases the inhabitants who are not often bothered by anything but local traffic and enjoy the resulting quiet.

The population of Brasilia is quite varied. Coming from all regions of Brazil, its inhabitants have put down their roots there. The veterans who lived through the period of construction proudly proclaim their seniority; and those who have recently moved to the capital are pleased to have left the noise and bustle of Rio or Sao Paulo for a calmer life. The absence of human contact is one reason why some people dislike the new capital, but in spite Brasilia remains a source of national pride.

For a long time they suffered from a lack of leisure and everything which adds life and excitement to a city. Today Brasilia has been transformed. Its clubs on the lake are full on Sundays; many country homes are now found in the region around the Federal District; and the capital's inhabitants are beginning to enjoy nature. In Brasilia everyone is proud of showing visitors the most famous building in Brazil, the Palacio da Alvorada, the residence of the President of Brazil. Its columns have become the capital's symbol.

Alvorada means dawn, a sign of hope in the future: Brasilia is quite definitely the image of a young nation full of optimism.

Preceding pages: View from
Corcovado on the lagoon and
the districts of Ipanema
and of Leblon.
Left: Copacabana, the name of
which symbolizes all the beaches
of Rio throughout the world.
Always present are the magnificent
sea, soft sand, sidewalks with
mosaic patterns forming waves,
and restaurants with their tables
under the palm trees.
Right: The center of Rio has
preserved much of the old
Portuguese city. In contrast, Rio
offers resolutely futuristic views
as modern Brazilian architecture
was born in the Brazilian
metropolis.

The population of Rio is one of the city's great tourist attractions: happy, relaxed, expansive, humming tunes and inventing funny stories, the people of Rio make contact easily, enjoy conversation and are always ready to open their hearts to strangers.

A succession of fabulous beaches
where you can swim throughout
the year, stretch out in the sun,
go surfing or just watch
the girls go by. A paradise for
doing nothing but also an essential
pivot of Rio's social life.

Preceding pages: A characteristic Rio view : the bridge over the bay connecting Rio with the city of Niteroi is 12 miles long, has six lanes of traffic and handles well over twenty thousand vehicles a day.

Colorful and incessant, Rio's activity is everywhere, in the streets as well as in the shops. The inhabitants of Rio are extremely hard-working although the pace of life in Rio sometimes gives the opposite impression.

A spectacle unique in the world: a soccer match at Maracana Stadium. Supporters, dressed in the colors of their team, wave flags and go wild when their team scores a point, singing rowdy songs.

The parade of the Samba Clubs during Carnival alone is worth the trip. An enchanting succession of disguises, acrobatic events, song and dance. The jury considers everything in choosing the best club of the year. A competitive spirit makes this event more sumptuous every year: a feast of music, color and laughter.

You should make two excursions, one to the top of Corcovado and the other to Sugar Loaf. The first can be done by car over a steep road through a forest or by cog railway which covers the 2,300 ft. in 20 minutes. The second, to Sugar Loaf, offers the thrill of cable cars: three minutes.

Up to Urca and an additional four minutes to the top of Sugar Loaf. Following pages: At an altitude of 1,320 ft. the splendor of a sight unique in the world. On the left, Copacabana and the ocean; in the middle, the Red Beach and Urca; and on the right, the bay, Botafogo and Flamengo.

*Left: Itamarati Palace ready for an official reception;
in the foreground, Bruno Giorgi's sculpture "The Meteor".
Right: The domes of the Chamber of Deputies and the
Senate in the center of the new capital.*

Oscar Niemeyer's architectural lyricism is well expressed in the Ministry of Foreign Affairs, on the left, as well as in the columns of

the Palace of the Plateau, on
the right. Brasilia is a poem of
colors, and a symphony of forms at
the conquest of space.

The Cathedral of Brasilia: 16 concrete V-shaped columns
132 ft. high rise skyward. Connecting the columns, clear
glass windows create inside the circular nave a poem of
light and shadow filled with forms moving with the sun.
Following pages: Sunset over the Square of the Three
Powers, the heart of a country turned toward the future.

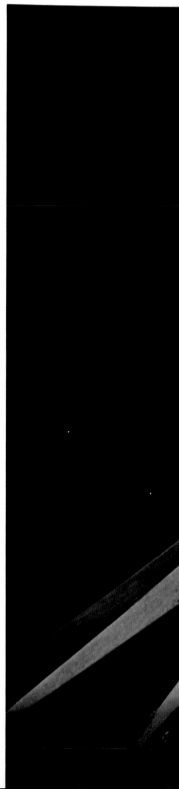

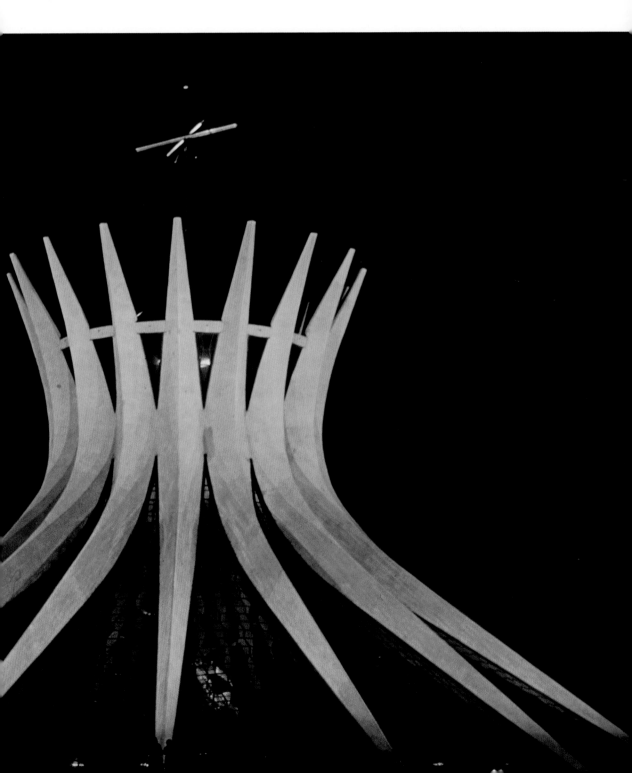

THE SOUTH

A plane leaves Rio for Sao Paulo every half hour. You need only go to the airport and buy a ticket for this shuttle service. Those who have more time will enjoy the trip by car or bus on the Via Dutra, an excellent road covering the 250 miles between the two cities over varied landscapes with a view of the magnificent Aqulhas Negras, the Black Needle Mountains.

The road along the water is even more beautiful. Between Rio and Santos it is filled with cliffs, coves, beaches, capes, islands, peninsulas and towns nestling between the Atlantic and a steep wall of mountains running along the coast. From Santos to Sao Paolo the road follows the trace of the route taken by the founders of the city four centuries ago.

Arriving in Sao Paolo, you will be surprised by the forest of shining skyscrapers. Sao Paolo is one of the fastest growing cities in the world and construction on a new building begins every 20 minutes. This spectacular vista of concrete and steel is best observed from the top of Morumbi, an elegant residential district south of the city or, in the center, from the top floor of the 41-storey Edificio Italia, the highest building in Sao Paolo.

Why did Sao Paolo, which will probably be bigger than Tokyo or New York in the year 2000, develop so fantastically from a city of 200,000 at the beginning of the century to more than 7 million at present ?

First because of coffee which was introduced at the beginning of the 19th century and was the basis of the Brazilian economy for many decades. The altitude of the plateau on which the city is built, the tropical climate and an abundance of terra roxa, the purple earth in which coffee flourishes, led to the development of coffee plantations. Virgin land was stripped, whole forests cleared to make room for these plantations, and railways built over lines known as the ``coffee route.'' The capital of the State of Sao Paolo consequently became an economic center.

The wealth of this city which initially came from the success of the coffee plantations has since been converted into industrial projects. Sao Paolo had 25 factories at the end of the 19th century; today more than 30,000 industrial establishments employing 800,000 workers, account for 50% of Brazil's industrial production. Sao Paolo became the leading industrial center in Latin America in only a few years. Its population increased with the emigration of Italians, Syrians, Japanese, Portuguese, Spaniards and others who have made Sao Paolo the cosmopolitan center of Brazil and decisively contributed to its incomparable growth. The city, in turn, has marked them with its life style and turned them all into proud *Paulistas,* inhabitants of Sao Paulo. The *Paulistas* have many reasons to feel proud. For instance, Sao Paulo has the highest per capita income and richest aggregate market in Brazil.

The city's rapid growth has created serious traffic problems and, although Sao Paolo now has its first subway line, traffic jams are frequent, as in all modern metropolises. The municipality is constantly opening new avenues, digging underground tunnels and building bridges and elevated highways, such as the Minhocao called the big worm, because of its curving form, in an attempt to overcome these traffic jams.

A drive around the city will expose you to bold futuristic urban planning concepts as well as to beautiful buildings. Sao Paolo has become the leading center of modern Brazilian architecture. Among the most impressive examples of this architecture are the Copan Building (in the form of an S), the new State Legislative Assembly and the Faculty of Architecture and Urbanism in the University City. Sao Paolo gives the appearance of a great museum, the works of which are scattered here and there.

Visits to factories are generally reserved for businessmen. But any tourist can appreciate the gigantic aspect of Sao Paolo by walking at night around the fine Municipal Market, the third largest in the world after those of New York and Paris. Ten thousand trucks deliver foodstuffs to it every day. For example, 35,000 tons of vegetables daily pass through this market and restaurants are found in adjacent streets serving onion soup, faithful to the tradition of such central markets.

The flower market, a gay, colorful spectacle, is held every day in the vegetable block. Growers of flowers display their wares and take orders but no one touches the flowers until the siren sounds. Then, and only then, are customers free to carry off their purchases.

Walking is a necessary part of seeing Sao Paolo as the city is an enormous stage. The street scene is continuous. Foreign tourists, thinking that they will find a homogeneous population in Brazil, will be fascinated by the multi-racial aspect of Sao Paolo. The city's always intense activity justifies its proud motto : ``Sao Paolo cannot stop''.

The European influence is still strong in the small farms where colonists from Northern Italy, Germany and Central Europe settled. They brought with them a life style completely different from that of the Brazilians who originally occupied the coastline in fortified villages after the period of the early Portuguese explorers. This melting pot in which later immigrant's traditions were blended with those of native or older Brazilians has produced an interesting and different regional way of life.

Men and women walking in the Rua Augusta and the Avenida Paulista are more elegant and sophisticated than those, more relaxed and colorful, at the Handcraft Fair held every Sunday on the Praça de República. Mingling with the crowd is an excellent way of making contact with the Paulistas. The international character of the city is also revealed by the number of excellent restaurants where the specialities of all cuisines in the world can be found.

Evening programs should include a visit to the samba clubs, night-clubs in which popular Brazilian music can be heard while sipping batidas, made of lemon or other fruit according to special, highly refined recipes. These clubs are open from 7 P.M. to the early hours of the morning. acões. Tudo é vidro e

Sao Paolo's growth has destroyed almost all traces of its past. Nonetheless, the city has preserved almost as a relic the 17th century Casa do Bandeirante at Praça Moteiro Lobato, the reconstructed home of a pioneer 350 years ago with its sugar cane mill, oven for bread and water hammer.

The former Convento da Luz contains a museum of sacred art. Its collection of colonial gold and silver, the most important of its kind in Brazil, stand out among the hundreds of sculptures, paintings and pieces of furniture shown in the corridors and monk's cells of this old monastery.

Renoir, Van Gogh, El Greco, Goya, Holbein, Bosch, Rembrandt and many other famous names are to be found in the catalogue of the Sao Paulo Art Museum, called by Paulistas "the youngest of the great museums in the world." The museum is located in a building standing on piles, facing one of the most beautiful vistas in the city. The interior has no walls or moulding but is made of glass and is filled with light so that the paintings seem to float in space. The names of the painter and data on the painting are placed on the rear of each work.

Works by Picasso, Braque, Dufy, Miro, Chagall, Kandinsky and Picabia are part of the collection of the Museum of Contemporary Art in Ibirapuera Park. The museum, where the most important modern art show in Latin America, the Sao Paolo Biennial, is held every two years alternately with the Venice Biennial, is alone worth a visit to Sao Paolo.

You can easily find the Parque Anhembi, the largest exhibition hall in Latin America covering more than 800,000 sq. ft. Thousands of arrows in the city indicate the way and publicize the events taking place. The Parque Enhembi is especially crowded during the Household Arts Show, the Auto Show and the Children's Show. Its steel structure is impressively bold and light.

Universally famous, the Butanta Institute is the most popular tourist attraction in Sao Paolo. Although its activities are quite varied (production of vaccine, genetic research, etc.), it is internationally known for its production of serum against the bites of snakes and spiders. Visitors may visit the snake farm and watch venin being taken from snakes, a sight which gives you the chills. You may even be fortunate enough to watch a mucurana, a big non-poisonous snake, devour a jararaca, one dose of whose poison is enough to kill ten people!

A visit to Sao Paolo is not complete without a trip to the coast, the port of Santos and the beaches of Guarujá. Two roads connect Sao Paolo with the ocean, the Via Anchieta and the new Via dos Imigrantes; both twist and turn down the forested escarpment of the Serra do Mar, and pass throught tunnels and over bridges, giving fantastic views of Santos and neighboring resorts. The two roads are the economic lifeline of Sao Paolo's industrial activity and the escape route for happy weekends on beaches.

Roads lead out of Sao Paulo in all directions and planes fly from its airports to all points in Brazil. Jets leave Sao Paolo daily for non-stop flights of an hour and a half to the Iguaçu Falls, perhaps the most overwhelming sight in South America and the high point of any trip to Brazil.

When she visited the Iguaçu Falls, Eleonor Roosevelt is reported to have exclaimed: "Poor Niagara!" In fact its height is greater than Niagara's, 235 ft. compared with 167 ft. In addition, the water of Iguaçu comes hurtling out of a virgin forest and its setting of begonias, orchids, ferns and palms with clouds of magnificently colored butterflies fluttering above is majestically beautiful Victoria Falls on the Zambezi River in Africa is higher (350 ft.), but, as the water falls into a narrow rocky fault, the effect is less impressive than that at Iguaçu.

Iguaçu means great waters in Guarani, the language of the Tupi-Guaranian people of Bolivia, Paraguay and southern Brazil. Above the main falls the Iguaçu River, which separates Brazil and Argentina, opens out to a width of 2 1/2 miles. This impressive mass of water plunges over a horseshoe-shaped precipice into a canyon; above the impact on the basalt rock of this deep canyon, the Devil's Throat (Garganta del Diablo), hover enormous clouds of spray, laced with magnificent blazing rainbows completely obscuring the bottom.

The falls should be seen from both the Argentinian and Brazilian sides to admire the spectacular views fully. General opinion seems to be that you can see the whole falls from Brazil only but that the partial views from Argentina are much more spectacular. In addition, a series of catwalks lead over the river all the way to the Devil's Throat.

However, the most thrilling experience on either side is a canoe trip along the upper reaches of the river and into the water about to plunge into the Devil's Throat. This surging mass of water, readying to rush headlong over the precipice, has a terrifying effect, the force of creation in its pure state and an effective hymn to nature.

However, such emotion is somewhat artificial. The canoe trip is totally without risk as it is offered only when conditions are right, that is when the river's level is low enough to be quite safe. Local inhabitants have been known to swim as far as the edge of the falls!

This fantastic sight can be admired from helicopter flights over the falls. The Hotel Cataratas on the Argentinian side, the only hotel just in front of the falls, offers flights for its guests. Varig jets taking off for Sao Paolo generally fly over the falls twice so that all passengers have a complete view of it. If they flew over only once, all the passengers might rush to the windows on one side, upsetting the plane's balance.

The three states comprising Southern Brazil, Paraná, Santa Catarina and Rio Grande do Sul, have a number of common characteristics which make this region quite different from the rest of the country. The relief of the mountains, the temperate climate (with sporadic snow storms in the winter), the presence of descendants of Polish, German and Italian immigrants, and the type of homes all contribute to endowing these states with a European atmosphere.

In the State of Rio Grande do Sul the mountains yield to immense stretches of pampas, the great grasslands stretching as far as Uruguay to the South and Argentina to the west and occupied by cattlemen since colonial times. The land has produced one of the most characteristic types of Brazilian, the gaucho, or cowboy, who spends the greater part of his life riding off into endless horizons.

Such diversity strikes visitors arriving in Porto Alegre and strolling on its busiest street, the Rua dos Andradas. The capital of Rio Grande do Sul, the city is the largest in the region and one of the most prosperous in the country. Half-way between the mountains in the north colonized by immigrants and the cattle land stretching southwest and inhabited by gauchos, Porto Alegre is marked by these two influences; and no one is surprised to see next to each other bombachas, the baggy pants worn by gauchos, and Tyrolian hats worn by the descendants of the German immigrants; or wine and beer, and Ximarão, maté tea without sugar.

A trip by boat on the Guaíba River providing an excellent general view of Porto Alegre will take you under the drawbridge connecting the capital with the southern part of the state. Four shafts are used to raise its apron to a height of 66 ft. above the water for the passage of tankers. Beautiful views of the city can also be had from the Morro Teresópolis and the TV Promontory.

Going north from Porto Alegre, the road leads through the hilly Serra Gaucha, the slopes of which are covered with vineyards. Caxias do Sul, Garibaldi and Bento Gonçalves in the mountains are three of Brazil's most important wine-producing centers. The wine cellars are open to visitors who are shown the various steps in wine-making. Grape and wine festivals during which wine and food flow freely are held from time to time throughout the year.

Two small charming towns close to each other in the mountains are garden spots, Canela and Gramado. When the hydrangeas bloom in the spring, Canela and Gramado seem covered in a mantle of white and blue. The houses of these two towns, most of which are wooden chalets, blend harmoniously into the surrounding landscape.

The Caracol National Park is a forest of pine trees with one of the highest falls in the world, the Caracol Cascade, 432 ft. high. From an observation point overlooking the falls you can admire the softly falling water turning into vapor before it reaches the bottom of the falls.

Further north you will discover another phenomenon of nature, the breathtaking canyon of Taimbezinho, a relatively narrow 14-mile long fault 1,650 ft. deep. It is so steep that the animals grazing close to the canyon sometimes slip and fall into it if they come too close to its edge.

Reaching the top of the canyon is a thrilling experience. If you are a sportsman, you may want to descend to its bottom covered by a mass of rocks piled up over the centuries. There you will hear only the sound of a brook in a rocky bed; overhead a narrow band of sky can be seen between rock walls.

An hour's flight takes you from Porto Alegre to Santo Angelo from which you can visit São Miguel, an 18th century fortified Jesuit monastery built to protect the Indians in the region. Preserved in a small neighboring museum, the bell which tolled three centuries ago is now silent forever but the chanting of the Guarani Indians seems still to echo through the monastery. The columns, capitals, arcades and facades indicate a high degree of civilization attained by the Indians under the missionaries.

When the lands of South America were divided between Spain and Portugal by the Treaty of Tordessillas, the Rio Grande do Sul became Spanish. It took two centuries for the Brazilian gauchos to reconquer this territory from the Spanish, and their descendants today are very proud of this.

The first gauchos were cattle herders from Sao Paulo. Then, later, they were joined by Portuguese immigrants from the Azores. Together with the

Indians, they fought ferociously to defend the land and are deeply attached to it. Riding across the pampas, they are accustomed to see far ahead and to be seen from afar. This accounts for their haughty bearing and their courage in hand-to-hand fighting.

Unlike the Argentina pampas, which are flat, the pampas of Rio Grande do Sul are formed of coxilhas, undulating prairies covered with grassland and interspersed with small woods and rivers. Bagé, Alegrete and Uruguaiana, the important towns in the region, are easily reached by plane.

Visits to cattle ranches are easy to arrange. The gauchos are very courteous and friendly although somewhat reserved due to the influence of the climate. The winters are very cold; and, when the minuano wind blows, there is nothing to do except remain by the fire and close all doors.

Although traditions are being lost everywhere in the world, many gauchos still wear their traditional clothes: baggy trousers, big spurs, a leather belt with a revolver and a long knife, a piece of leather on the leg as protection against the friction of the lasso, a neck scarf, a long whip in the right hand often used on the cattle, a woolen poncho as protection against the rain and wind. Their saddles are covered in sheepskin to keep them warm and soft.

The favorite drink of the gaucho is Ximarão, maté tea without sugar kept in a small round pot which passes from hand to hand and is sipped by all through the same silver straw. When the pot is empty, they add some maté tea and three litres of water.

Ximarão is difficult to drink if you are not accustomed to it. Churrasco, which is barbecued meat roasted over the heat of charcoal in the open air and seasoned only with salt, is a gaucho creation prepared in the open by gauchos using only their long knives and now considered a national dish. You help yourself, somewhat dazzled by the different kinds of grilled meat, to piles of skewers placed on tables.

The gauchos also hold rodeos from time to time, and give spectacular demonstrations of calf roping and bronco riding. The most important is held in Vacaria every two years. Wild horses are brought into the corral; the gauchos pin them down by seizing their ears and mouth. The contestants mount them bareback and grasp their mane. The horse is set free and the cow boys begin to fall off left and right. Only a few contestants are able to hang on to the other side of the ring where they leap over another gaucho and receive the applause of the audience.

Traditions and folklore are maintained in all towns of the Rio Grande do Sul by Centers of Gaucho Traditions. The variety of dancing, the beautiful costumes and the gay music provide an incomparable sight. Some dances are executed by men only and give the cowboys a pastime while around a camp fire in the pampas at night, such as the fast, rhythmical dance of the knives and the chula with its acrobatic steps danced on either side of a stick on the ground. These virile dances exalt the soul of a people who have conquered the land by the force of work, defended it with blood and continue to cherish it above all with much tenderness and passion.

*Preceding pages: A bridge on the Rio-São Paulo
highway at the foot of the Aqulhas Negras, the Black
Needle Mountains, symbol of a young country.
Opposite and below: Contrasting with the skyscrapers
and traffic jams of São Paulo's center, a residential
district with its gardens, small havens of quiet.*

The center of São Paulo on a week day. The rapid growth of the city creates serious problems and traffic jams are frequent, as in all large cities in the world. Boulevards are built, tunnels are dug and bridges and elevated highways are opened in an attempt to solve some of the many problems of the city.

Below: The São Paulo Art Museum, "the youngest of the great museums in the world." The interior has no walls or moulding; everything is glass and light. Right: The monument of the Bandeirantes by Victor Brecheret, a tribute to the glory of colonial pioneers.

The rapid development of São Paulo was initially due to coffee (center) and then to industry (top and right). At the end of the 19th century, São Paulo had 25 factories; today there are more than 30,000, from which comes more than 50% of Brazil's total production.
Below: Extracting venom from a jararaca at the Butanta Institute, known throughout the world for its production of vaccine against snake and spider bites.

*Top left: Taimbezihno Canyon, a relatively
narrow 14-mile long fault 1,650 ft. high.
Lower left: Caracol Cascade, 432 ft. high; its water
vaporizes before reaching the bottom of the falls.
Below: Porto Alegre reflected in the Guaiba River.*

The ruins of São Miguel Monastery, the last vestige of
the Seven Villages founded by the Jesuits in the 17th
century to protect the Guarani Indians. The columns,
capitals and arcades indicate a high degree of civilization
reached by the Indians under the missionaries.
Following pages: Gauchos in the pampas with their
sheep and cattle, churrasco and chimarrão.

Iguaçu Falls, one of the marvels of the world. The river separating Brazil and Argentina opens out to a width of 2 1/2 miles above the main falls. This mass of water plunges into a canyon with a width of less than 330 ft, forming a horseshoe consisting of 21 falls. Most of the falls plunge downward in two stages (below) but in the center the water falls in a single span into the Devil's Throat, more than 200 ft. below (opposite).

MINAS GERAIS

If you fly from Rio to Brasilia, you should stop in Belo Horizonte. The plane fare is the same since the city is on the route to the Brazilian capital, and there are many flights. If travelling by car or bus, you can agreeably break the trip by stopping in the capital of Minas Gerais, the third largest city in Brazil and well worth a visit.

Although it has no outlet on the sea, the State of Minas Gerais is one of the richest in Brazil.

The inland state of Minas Gerais is about the size of Texas and mainly situated on the Brazilian central plateau. The southern part of the state is mountainous and the north contains undulating grazing land. Minas Gerais is the state which produces the most beans, corn and garlic. It is the second most important states in terms of production of rice, bananas, tea and oranges and comes third in production of coffee, sugar and tobacco. It also produces cotton and grapes.

In addition, almost all of Brazil's iron ore, bauxite, graphite and mica come from the state as well as a large percentage of its manganese, beryllium, industrial diamonds, chromium and rock crystal. Minas Gerais also contains the only two gold mines still mined in Brazil.

Nothing at the beginning of the colonial period indicated that it would play an important rôle in the history of the country.

It all began in the 17th century when tireless gold and diamond prospectors found fabulously rich finds. A gold rush in the 18th century preceded the gold rushes of California and South Africa. The gold mines made prospectors, as well as the Kings of Portugal, rich in the 18th century; the prospectors were obliged to pay the king a 20% tax on the gold found. So much gold was mined that the capital of Brazil was transferred from Bahia to Rio de Janeiro in 1763 in order to check more closely on such a source of wealth.

The first gold nuggets were discovered by chance in a stream among small black rocks which had to be crushed. Then prospectors began to flood the slopes of the mountain and separate the gold from the mud by the process of decantation; and once the surface wealth was exhausted, they began to dig mines in the mountains.

The King remained the owner of all underground wealth. Gold mining was authorized through concessions and the sites well plotted out. Adventurers going off into deserted regions also obtained permission to prospect for gold. But all had to pay a fifth of the gold found to the Royal Treasury. Prospectors obviously tried by all means to hide the amount of gold which they really found and the treasury had difficulty in imposing its rights. Various remedies were tried to solve this situation, all of which led to the foundry system requiring that all gold mined had to be presented to be weighed and melted into bars marked with the royal seal. Trade in gold powder or nuggets was consequently forbidden and subject to severe punishment including confiscation of one's property and exile to Africa.

The sources of this gold eventually were exhausted; and with them disappeared a frantic, adventurous kind of life. A pastoral economy resumed its former importance and the State of Minas Gerais once more became prosperous because of its cattle. However, its name was again to be justified with the discovery of iron, so much of which was found so quickly that the assistance of foreign capital had to be sought. The earliest foreign investors were Belgian and the most recent Japanese. The steel industry has consequently given the region a second prosperity also based on the sub-soil.

We might have said "soil" as the mountains around Belo Horizonte are gray because of the amount of iron on the surface of the ground. An incalculable fortune awaits the inventor of a profitable means of extracting the iron from this earth. At present, if the metal is ever used in blast furnaces, the mass of earth around it will prevent firing. Industrial extraction of iron is therefore concentrated on the mines where the iron ore content per ton is much higher.

Belo Horizonte, the capital of Minas Gerais and the third largest city in Brazil, stands at an altitude of 2,500 ft above sea level. It has a great many German and Italian settlers and is a mining and agricultural center as well as a city of developing industry depending on local minerals, especially iron and manganese used in the production of steel. The capital's heavy industry is located in a valley just outside the city. Belo Horizonte is also a diamond cutting center, and trade in amethysts, topazes and agates mined in Minas Gerais is brisk.

Belo Horizonte is proud of having been in 1893 one of the first cities in the world to be planned. Inspired by L'Enfant's plan for Washington, D.C., the rectangular grid pattern of its streets is cut by diagonal avenues and corresponded to avant-garde city planning at the time. The plan unfortunately overlooked the irregular nature of the site's relief. Since the site is not flat, the streets were built with steep slopes in order to follow the plan.

Nature gradually recovered its rights. The railroad, built without reference to the map, followed the trace of the curves which the site required. The city, which grew rapidly and was freed from its initial restraint, is today a metropolis of a million and a half inhabitants where life is pleasant and the climate always fine. The last ransom which Belo Horizonte has paid to the futuristic plan of 1893 is its triangular buildings, which are not without elegance, and are built at diagonal crossings in order to benefit from a maximum of land.

Not far from the city on the shores of Lake Pampulha, Oscar Niemeyer built some of his earliest buildings, the casino now used as a museum, and the Chapel of São Francisco decorated by the painter Cândido Portinari. Pampulha, a sports center, has a yacht club and a soccer stadium holding 130,000 spectators, one of the biggest in Brazil.

The prehistoric caves of Lapinha and Maquiné, north of Belo Horizonte and both 1,650 ft. long, are well worth a visit. For thousands of years, nature has patiently sculpted beautiful and strange stalactites now enhanced with a new type of beauty by modern lighting. The caves were explored in 1845 by the Danish naturalist Lund who discovered the fossil of a primitive man 8 1/4 ft. high at Lapinha. The two caves can easily be visited on the same day despite the distance between them as they are both on the same paved road leading from Belo Horizonte.

Ouro Preto is an hour and half by car from Belo Horizonte. The capital of the State of Minas Gerais until the end of the last century and former center of mining in Brazil, Ouro Preto is now a national monument. Rising like a dream, it conjures up an impression of the past like no other town in the world, except Toledo and Assisi.

It was originally called Vila Rica, the rich town. The mud houses formed eleven districts, one of which, Ouro Preto, the most important parish seat, finally became the name of the town.

Ouro Preto maintained its original aspect during the first half of the 18th century, contrasting with the wealth from gold, the mining of which was then at its zenith. Only in 1740 were stone buildings first built; the fortress-like Governor's Palace, for example, dating from 1741, houses, bridges, fountains, chapels and churches. As it is today Ouro Preto has the most harmonious complex in all of America of houses built during the mid-18th century, the period of its great splendor.

And what splendor! Unlike Manaus, the opulence of which due to rubber was personified in 1900 by performances of opera and bottles of champagne imported from Europe, the prosperity of Ouro Preto created an original culture. The region had its own literary school, architectural style, current of political thought (which was the first to advocate Brazil's independence) and school of music.

The gold was gradually exhausted and the brilliant society of Ouro Preto disappeared. The capital of the State of Minas Gerais was transferred to Belo Horizonte in 1897 as the mountain site of Ouro Preto was impractical in terms of modern development. The years passed without changing its ancient aspect. Classified a national monument in 1933, Ouro Preto remains almost intact, barely touched by the transformations of progress.

Many tourists limit their visit to Ouro Preto to a day excursion and return to Belo Horizonte. This is a pity as you should spend at least a night there in order to experience the overwhelming poetry of the town. There are many good hotels, some of which—highly recommended— are located in old mansions. A stroll through the silent streets in the evening provides an unforgettable contact with history in the company of the specters of the past.

These ghosts include, among others, the young poet Tomas Antonio Gonzaga, who declaimed verses to his beloved Maria Doroteia de Seixas, whom he called by the sweet name Marilia. Tomas passionately loved his country and was among a group of conspirators urging the liberation of Brazil from Portugal. Betrayed with his fellow revolutionaries, he was exiled to Africa. As he left, chanting his despair in fine verses, the leader of the conspiration, Tiradentes, a national hero, was being hanged. The specter of Tiradentes is also present in the streets of Ouro Preto.

From the hill of Santa Efigênia, a black Nubian queen who was canonized by the Catholic Church, descend the ghosts of her fellow brothers, the subjects of Chico Rei, a powerful sovereign conquered with his people and taken into slavery. Chico Rei bought back his freedom through hard work, and then gradually that of his compatriots. He had the church of his patron saint built with a fountain at its entrance where black women washed their hair on holidays. The gold powder with which they decorated themselves fell to the bottom of the fountain and was in turn used to buy back the liberty of other slaves.

The last ghost is that of Antonio Francisco Lisboa, a modest, miserable man who was sick, died ignored and entered history as a great artist. Known as O Aleijadinho (the little cripple), a nickname filled with tenderness, he sculpted doors, fountains, chairs and medallions and built the lovely church of São Francisco de Assis, revealing that he was also a great architect as well as a great sculptor.

There are so many churches in Ouro Preto that it is difficult to take a photo of the town without including two or three of them. The many religious brotherhoods in the 18th century were often rivals, each brotherhood wanting to have its own church. The work sites multiplied; and sincere rivalry motivated builders to try to excel each other through the ornamentation and beauty of their works. All brotherhoods were involved in building churches: brotherhoods of governors, the people, the whites, the blacks, the rich and the poor. This collective effort created the magnificent sanctuaries of Ouro Preto. This was probably the last time in history that an entire people was mobilized for such a cause and this effort has been referred to as "the last generation of cathedrals".

You should prepare an itinerary for visiting the churches as some are open in the morning and others in the afternoon. And although the distances are short, the hills are quite steep. You should first do a dry run on the circuit by car and then walk through the maze of streets to enjoy and feel the town's atmosphere.

We recommend that you visit all twelve churches of Ouro Preto, even the poorest, as you will appreciate the rich decoration of the others even more.

In any event, you should see five of these churches, the two parish churches of Antonio Dias and the Igreja do Pilar, the Carmo Church of São Francisco de Assis and the chapel of Padre Faria with its magnificent altar, a short distance from the other churches.

Two churches derserve a visit because of their exceptional view of the town, the church of Santa Efigênia with a view over the eastern part of Ouro Preto and the church of São Francisco do Paulo with a view over the western side of town framed by high peaks on the horizon.

After the churches you will want to visit the civil monuments. On the Praça Tiradentes, two buildings face each other, the Governor's Palace, today the School of Mines, built by Aleijadinho's father, and the former Town Hall now containing the museum of the Inconfidentes, the revolutionaries who planned the revolt against Portuguese domination in 1788. Lower down in the square is the Casa das Contas, the house of contrasts, a beautiful home built by a rich merchant and confiscated in 1802 because of debts owed the royal treasury.

You should also wander around Ouro Preto, discovering a fountain here, a lovely wood balcony there and an unexpected view further on; crossing the stones over which' gold prospectors once walked; admiring the soapstone facades of the churches; and watching a timeless sunset filled with the poetry and beauty of a vision.

Congonhas do Campo, a small hill town, is 35 miles south of Ouro Preto on the Rio-Belo Horizonte highway. A September fiesta in its church swells the population of the town from 18,000 to 250,000. In the gold age Congonhas do Campo was already famous. The town was dominated by the great pilgrimage church of Bom Jesus dos Matozinhos. Below its terrace are six small chapels set in sloping gardens, recalling the 18th century religious gardens of Braga in Portugal, with life-size carved Passion figures. Fortunately, Aleijadinho was the sculptor of these figures!

Antonio Francisco Lisboa began these statues in 1796. He was then 57 and had already developed the terrible disease which atrophied his hands, paralyzed his feet, and forced him to work in a kneeling, and ultimately prone, position with his hammer and chisel strapped to his wrists. Sublimating his suffering, he created one of his masterpieces. The baroque style, which had degenerated into a pretentiously formalistic style in Europe, found in Aleijadinho a new strong and lyrical breath.

The six chapels in which scenes of the Passion are represented and are arranged on a slope leading to the church. They contain 66 statues but only the main works are by Aleijadinho; the secondary figures are by his students who also did the first wood sketches of these works.

The face of the soldiers are deliberately grotesque and those of the apostles express surprise, fear and incomprehension. Saint Peter is asleep, and even dreaming, on the Mount of Olives; the weeping women of Jerusalem on the way of the Cross are overwhelmingly touching and dignified; even more admirable are the faces of Jesus expressing the development of suffering from the serene study of the Last Supper to the pain of the Crucifixion.

However incredible it may appear, the 19th century was unable to recognize the value of these sculptures which were retouched to such an extent that they became almost unrecognizable. A long restoration project has succeeded in scraping off the layers of paint and restoring the works to their original color. Paradoxically, however, the unfortunate retouching preserved the original paint from the wear and tear of time, keeping it intact until now.

Twelve prophets carved in soapstone stand on the parapets of the church's terrace. Antonio Francisco Lisboa attained the summit of his art in these works: Jonas raises his head to the sky and pleads for God's mercy; at his feet the whale breathes; Ezechiel looks afar beyond the mountains and even beyond centuries, thrown to the ground and watching the Last Judgment; Isaiah with his impressive beard expresses fatigue as well as the lucid quietude of old age; and Daniel, a lion at his feet, exalts the force and beauty of youth.

The statues are not aligned with each other but beautifully arranged on the terrace. Several of the prophets look at each other; others are haughtily gesticulating. The movement of the group changes as you move about. The statues seemingly come to life in front of the church as do the pilgrims, the mountain, and the future which the eyes of the prophets contemplate. With this level of genius, these works are not merely twelve sculptures but a moment in eternity forever seized in stone.

Other towns in Minas Gerais have conserved remnants of their past splendor —for instance São Joao del Reil, Tiradentes, Diamantina, Catas Altas, Santa Barbara and Caeté.

Two can be visited on the way to Ouro Preto. Cachoeira do Campo has a fine church and Mariana a remarkable town hall in addition to its churches.

Sabara is only 15 miles from the center of Belo Horizonte and, if time permits, should be part of your itinerary. An old town with simple houses, it has one of the oldest theaters in Brazil, today used as a movie house, but its marvelous interior decoration has fortunately not been touched.

The church of Nossa Senhora da Conceiçao, finished around 1714, is one of the oldest churches in Minas Gerais. Its rustic facade contrasts with the opulence of the church of Nossa Senhora do Carmo decorated by Aleijadinho. A visit to these two churches is an excellent means of appreciating the evolution of the baroque style in this region throughout the 18th century.

The jewel of Sabara is the chapel of Nossa Senhora do O, which alone is worth a visit to the town and which is decorated with painted wood panels several of which have Chinese motifs. These panels were probably done by Portuguese artists who had been in Macao. The chapel was built in 1725 and has not been touched since.

You should not leave Sabara without visiting the museum of gold mining in the ancient Intendencia de Ouro where the gold was melted before being taxed. The museum displays the original tools used by the early prospectors in panning gold, models of old devices used in mining gold, and a model of the Morro Velho gold mine where gold is still being mined.

Diamantica, once the center of an active diamond industry, is perhaps the most interesting and least spoiled of Brazil's colonial mining towns. Its excellent colonial remains include churches and houses with beautifully carved overhanging roofs. The house of Chica Da Silva, an 18th century mulatto slave who married a diamond prospector and became a folk heroine, is at Praça Lobo Mesquita 266. The diamond Museum in the house of Prade Robim who was involved in the plot for independance in 1789, is also worth a visit. Serro, not far from Diamantina, is also an unspoiled colonial town with six beautiful baroque churches, fine squares and a museum. Diamantina and Serro can be reached from Belo Horizonte over a road running through a rocky landscape.

You may experience a touch of melancholy once you have left the historical towns of Minas Gerais and resumed your place in the modern world. This is due to nostalgia for a lost past, for a period when life was more peaceful and the search for fortune did not exclude a thirst for beauty.

Belo Horizonte, one of the first cities to be planned, was
built in 1893. The rectangular grid pattern of its streets
was avant-garde for the period and explains the
triangular buildings found at the intersections of its
diagonally crossing avenues and thoroughfares.
Following pages: Ouro Preto, Brazil's town-museum.

Belo Horizonte succeeded
Ouro Preto as the state
capital in 1897 and, since,
the years have passed
without any change in the
town's exterior aspect.
Ouro Preto was classified
a national monument in
the nineteen thirties.

Ouro Preto, the former capital of the State of Minas Gerais, has been preserved exactly as it was 200 years ago. Its prosperity favored the flowering of a brilliant culture which disappeared when the gold mines were completely exhausted.

In the square before the Church of Congonhas do Campo, the 12 prophets carved in sandstone by Antonio Francisco Lisboa. In these sculptures Lisboa reached the height of his art. Crippled by a disease which paralyzed his feet and atrophied his hands, he had to work in a kneeling or prone position with his hammer and chisel strapped to his wrists. He sublimated his suffering by creating these masterpieces and has passed into the history of Art under the name af Aleijadinho.

Following pages: The prehistoric caves of Lapinha and Maquine provide an impressive trip through prehistory. For thousands of years, nature has patiently sculpted beautiful, strange stalactites now enhanced by an elaborate display of modern lighting.

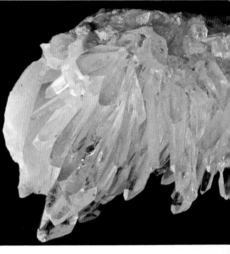

BAHIA

Salvador, or Bahia, as it is often called, was the first city founded in Brazil and remained its capital for more than 200 years. Now the fifth largest city in the country, Salvador is the capital of the State of Bahia. An urban area of contrasting skyscrapers in its center and huts in old fishing communities, the city also has its fair share of old colonial houses near the port. Old Salvador is a living monument to the splendour of baroque art.

Salvador is the center of Brazil's tobacco trade and is famous for its mild cigars. It also exports coffee, hides, waxes, cocoa and sugar. Salvador's atmosphere is more relaxed than that of Rio: the local people are very slow and quiet in their speech, attitude and gestures. The beauties and joys of Salvador can best be discovered and enjoyed if you adapt yourself to this relaxed manner of living.

The tempo is much slower than in Rio and there is far less traffic and bustle in the streets. The city, over a thousand miles from Rio, has a population of more than a million inhabitants. For many Brazilians it is a favorite vacation spot. Its 40 miles of white sandy beaches, blue sea and skies, and coconut groves are the chief attractions for those choosing Salvador as a site for their vacations. It rains throughout the year (in Salvador) but April, May and September are the wettest months when it may drizzle for several days in a row or be cloudlessly clear, fresh and cool.

When you have had enough of sunny beaches and endless expanses of clean sand, you can visit the cool museums in the city where you can see wood carvings, silver and gold reliquaries, icons, colonial furniture and other objects from the past. This same past is never absent from the streets, the old colonial houses around Pillory Lane and the beautiful colonial churches which contrast with Salvador's modern skyscrapers and crowded overpasses.

Most liners from the United States or Europe stopped in Bahia on their way to Rio until quite recently; and passengers had a chance to admire the view of Salvador from the sea. Flying to Salvador, you miss this unique view but as compensation you drive over an incredibly beautiful road between the airport and the city.

This road first passes through a fishing village, a popular theme of many Brazilian songs, with a lovely beach, the first in a succession of unforgettable stretches of sand—Itapoa, Piata, Boco do Rio, Armacao, Pituba, Amaralina, Rio Vermelho and Ondina, all with very fine white sand shaded by coconut trees crowning the turquoise ocean and filled with happy, sunburned bathers.

This lovely seascape ends in new boulevards, tunnels and bridges leading directly into the heart of the modern city of Salvador just beyond which lies the old city, the essence of Brazil's charm and its very heart.

The first to discover this exceptional site was André Gonçalves at the head of an expedition which reached the bay of Rio two months later. He arrived on the site of Bahia on 1 November 1501 and gave the wide bay the name of that feast day, the Bahia de Todos os Santos (Bay of All Saints).

The town was founded in 1549 by Tomé de Souza, the first governor-general of Brazil, as the colonial capital in the middle of the long coastal expanse of land which he had to defend. The town had to be protected and the Portuguese built fortresses at strategic points the outlines of which still form important landmarks.

Salvador was the capital of Brazil for 214 years. Architecture and trade, letters and economy, the plastic arts and patriotism all prospered here together. Rio de Janeiro became the capital in 1763 and Bahia entered a dormant period lasting a century and a half. But today Salvador is being reborn in a rush of activity. The industrial center of Aratu, petroleum refineries, trade and tourism indicate that a new phase in its history has opened.

The word "Bahia", written in Portuguese with an "h", administratively refers not to a city but to one of Brazil's states the capital of which is Salvador. However, "baia" means bay and is therefore applied to the Bay of All Saints. In addition, as the capital has become the symbol of the entire state, the name "Bahia" has come indiscriminately to designate the state, the capital and the bay in front of which the latter was built.

The town was built on a peninsula for strategic purposes easy to understand, facing the interior with its back to the sea. It first developed along the beach, then reached the mountain behind and began to sprawl all the way to the top. This has led to the division of the city into the Baixa (lower part) and Alta (upper part). As it grew, the city began to cover the entire peninsula and new districts along the beaches have recently been created.

You will need at least three days to visit the historical part of Salvador. Tourists will do well to alternate sightseeing with relaxing on the beach because of the tropical heat and steep streets. There is certainly enough in Salvador to keep you very busy and happy.

Of all the sites you may decide to visit—the most ornate church, the most beautiful cloister or the most extraordinary collection of tiles, the most fantastic is the Franciscan monastery with its 18th century church.

Why dedicate a gold church to Saint Francis, the helper of the poor? Because baroque artists wanted the sanctuary to be a reflection of heaven and tried to give the faithful an impression of ecstasy and an image of paradise. The church of São Francisco de Assis is not, in any event, the most ornate in Brazil as the gold leaf on the carved woodwork is very thin. Its interest lies rather in the "talha" wood carved to reflect light off of flat surfaces. Go to Saint Francis for evening mass when the gold shines the most: the sight is impressive.

The cloister of the monastery is covered with tiles offered by King John V of Portugal and representing Horace's maxims, a very popular subject at that time. You should take the time to study each scene—in order to discover its meaning, analyze the characters and appreciate the details. This anthology of customs includes an old man with glasses, a sick man whose eyes are being operated on and a miser counting his money.

The artistic treasures of the monastery also include the sacristy and the chapter house. Panels painted on the ceiling and the walls represent invocations of the Virgin's litanies. But the masterpiece is the exceptionally dramatic statue of Saint Peter of Alcantata unequalled in 18th century statuary, found in the central chapel of the church's right side aisle.

Along with the church of São Francisco, the Church of the Ordem Terceira (the Franciscan Third Order) has an exceptionally rich stone façade. This marvel remained for a long time hidden under layers of rough plaster until recently restored by the Historical Monuments Agency.

The Cathedral, an old Jesuit church dating from the second half of the 17th century, is on the other side of the square in front of the Church of São Francisco. It is less ornate but larger. Its gold-covered altars trace the evolution of the baroque style. The early altars have flat surfaces; those next in age begin to bear reliefs; and the most recent are flowerings of sculpture. Here again the strongest impression is in the evening when all the lights are shining; and this impression is extended into the large sacristy and to the remarkable sculpture of its rosewood panels.

The lyrics of a song claim that ''Bahia has 365 churches'', one for each day of the year. There are in fact not as many although the city does count more than 70. Don't miss the church of Nossa Senhora do Carmo with its silver altar and very beautiful sacristy. Or Nossa Senhora da Conceiçao da Praia in the lower city, brought stone by stone from Portugal. The stones were transported free of charge as the sculpted and numbered stones were used aş ballast for boats seeking colonial products.

The ancient convent of Saint Theresa houses the Sacred Art Museum containing a collection of 16th century sculpture, painting, silver and glazed tile panels as well as temporary items from other religious buildings. The arrangement enhances each object and the atmosphere is one of contemplation. This lesson in art is also a pleasure for the eye. The visit to the museum in the former Carmelite convent is a fitting complement to that of the Sacred Art Museum.

Continuing on to Itapagipe peninsula, you will discover one of the most beautiful views of the city as well as a beautiful architectural gem, the chapel of Monte Serrat which has among its treasures a splendidly naive terracotta statue of a repentant Saint Peter.

Not far from the chapel is the Church of Our Lord of Bonfim (or Good End), which is much less interesting artistically than the chapel but, nonetheless, has a very special place in the hearts of local inhabitants.

The most popular local religious festival is held once a year in January, the ritual of the washing of the Church of Our Lord of Bonfim. The inhabitants of Salvador once did actually wash the interior of the church but as the ceremony eventually came to end with a *candomblé* dance, washing was finally limited to the steps of the church. Today the number of people in the procession carrying vases full of water on their heads is too large for any washing ceremony. But this religious holiday has become a pretext for a joyous festival with music, dancing and attractions and an opportunity for fun in the streets.

Every January 1 the statue of Our Lord of Seafarers is taken by boat from a church on the waterfront at Boa Viagem, carried to another church and then returned to its home. This was once a very beautiful and meaningful ceremony:

the statue was embarked on a long row boat and carried over the water, escorted by a fleet of sail boats and canoes, back to Boa Viagem. Today the row boat takes off with the roar of an engine surrounded by other noisy, motor-driven outboards and the sail boats with their majestic sails, unable to follow any longer, wait, without moving for the return of the statue.

Progress has, however, given an added impetus to another festival, the Carnival. One fine day three adolescents placed a couple of loud speakers on a truck and drove through the streets playing music. A crowd began to follow them, singing and dancing: the first "electrical trio" was born. At present, trucks carrying 10, 15 or 20 musicians, are equipped with dozens of loud speakers although they are still referred to as "electrical trios". These "trios" have created a new kind of music and a different kind of atmosphere. The Bahia Carnival is beginning to supplant Rio's carnival because of this music and atmosphere if we can believe what we hear in the streets.

There are many festivals in Bahia throughout the year but the months of January and February, during which those which we have just mentioned are held, are the best time to visit Salvador. It is summer there at that time but the heat is more than bearable and there is no rain.

During the two centuries of Salvador's history as the capital of Brazil, the city was embellished with many *solares*, fine colonial mansions belonging to rich sugar cane plantation owners. Several of these old houses painted in shades of pink, yellow, blue and green can still be visited including the Solar do Unhao, the Solar do Sandaha, the home of Ruy Barbosa and the House of the Seven Chandeliers.

Two museums in Salvador provide a good idea of the former splendor of life in Bahia. The Museu do Costa Pinto contains an important private collection of period furniture, silver, jewels and art objects donated to the State in a particularly attractive location on the outskirts of the city; and the Museu do Recôncavo, a traditional Brazilian 16th century complex consisting of a sugar mill, a chapel and a manor house, displays items representing three centuries of economic, political and social life in Bahia.

Returning to Salvador, you pass through the industrial sector of Aratu, an area reserved for industrial development. Here you will find a contrasting landscape of big buildings and factory chimneys in the middle of a lush tropical forest with artificial lakes all around. The futuristic vision is even more striking at the hydroelectric plant of Paulo Afonso an hour by plane from Salvador. Here you can stay in a modern hotel and visit the dam and the turbine room dug out of the rock and as big as an underground cathedral.

After visiting the important artistic and historic points of interest in Salvador, you should just stroll through the streets and stop to admire a lovely architectural detail, enjoy a picturesque sight or find yourself on a small quiet square where children are playing soccer.

A Brazilian song has made the Baixa do Sapateiro, a crowded section, famous. The Largo do Pelourinho (Pillory Square) or the streets leading to the district around the Carmo Church are even more charming. The upper and lower city are connected by roads and public lifts. The conventional Lacerda elevator takes passengers up the 235 ft. rise from the Traça Cairu in the lower city to the Praça Municipal on the plateau; and the Gonçalves funicular brings passengers to its terminus behind the cathedral. A trip in either is more exciting if done without too much planning.

The exuberance of Salvador is felt best in the streets where a joyous feeling seemingly floats in the air and appears in the temperament of the inhabitants. Of all Brazilian cities, Salvador has the largest proportion of blacks, who have given the city an expansive air and a love for rhythm, color and sparkle. They have even created a characteristic Brazilian type, the Bahiana with her full, bright skirt and turban. The image of the Bahiana is so well established now that there is always a group of Bahianas in traditional costumes in the parade of the samba clubs during the Rio Carnival.

Items relating to the folklore of Bahia can be admired in the municipal museum located in one of the recently restored mansions on the Largo do Pelourhino in old Salvador.

Although the number of traditionally dressed Bahianas unfortunately decreases every year, many still prepare appetizing dishes of food which they sell in the streets. The most typical dish is *acarajé*, black bean balls fried in palm oil, stuffed with *vatapá* or shrimps and served with *cocada puxa-puxa*, hard *cocada* with peanuts, tapioca or *quindins*.

The cooking of Bahia is unjustly reputed to be heavy and difficult to digest. On the contrary, palm oil is easily digestible and a small portion of *vatapá* or *caruru* is easier on the stomach than *feijoada*. Pepper, however, should be used sparingly. Although a Bahiano invariably chooses the strongest pepper available and copiously seasons his food with it, two or three pinches of the weakest pepper is enough to burn the mouth of unsuspecting travellers.

As we have said, wherever you go in Salvador, you feel an African influence. Humor, food, folklore and dances are all inspired by African traditions. The most typical dance is the *Capoeira*, portraying a wrestling match. Formerly a mortal foot-fight in which the feet were used as effectively as the hands in karate, the *capoeira* was forbidden because of its violence and became a highly athletic dance to the sound of drum, tambourine and *berimbau*.

Young Bahianos master this dance in special schools where old teachers transmit the secret of their art, just as elsewhere the techniques of classical dance of fencing are taught. Folklore dancing is held every evening at the *samba de roda* and the *maculelê* is danced in addition to the *capoeira*.

Dancers also mime fishermen drawing in their nets, as on the beach, to an obsessive chanting rhythm. These colorful performances are more beautiful and authentic than demonstrations of *candomblê* for tourists.

Musicians accompany the *capoeira* on the *berimbau* ,a wooden bow with a steel bowstring held by a coin and played with a stick. You can buy this strange instrument at the Mercado Modelo (Model Market) in the old customs house built in 1861 on Praça Cairu.

This picturesque market deserves a long visit for its vivid strings of beads, hats, hammocks, leather jackets and such elegant gifts as tortoise-shell belts, bunches of grapes made of colored stones, and metal objects worn by the Bahanias since the colonial period as well as *balangandans*, brightly colored terracotta figurines, and tiny Bahiana figures with full skirts, beads and baskets of fruit on their head.

Saturday morning is the best day to visit the Mercado Modelo. The market is crowded and lively and an uninterrupted spectacle of improvised dances and *capoeiras* is held in the neighboring streets. The ideal place from which to watch this lively scene is from one of the bar or restaurant terraces where an incredible variety of *batidas*, a delicious and powerful drink made of exotic fruit and crude white rum, is served along with typically Bahiano food.

The São Joaquim Fair, equally typical, offers visitors piles of watermelon, pineapple and other fruit as well as large colored plates containing cloth dyes, herbs, spices and incense. Following an ancient custom, houses in Bahia are shut up every Saturday and perfumed with the fragrance of incense. The Feira de São Joaquim is a popular pottery market where jugs, pitchers, bowls and jars of all kinds are sold.

A pleasant, leisurely boat trip around the bay will give you a good chance to admire the view of Salvador. The bay is studded with small, unspoiled islands; Itaparica, the most famous, can be reached by a short boat ride of less than two hours and has excellent, quiet beaches.

The boats crossing the Bahia de Todos os Santos formerly went up the Paraguacu River as far as the town of Cachoeira from which the road inland used to branch out. Today this old town, 75 miles from Salvador, has lost its economic importance but has preserved intact the atmosphere and charm of a distant, prosperous age. Cachoeira can be easily reached now over a new paved road. Its old colonial mansions recall the past and the decorative details of the church of the Ordem Terceira do Carmo are exceptionally rich and harmonious.

A visit to Bahia should end in a dream as it began. Near the airport is the dark-green freshwater Abaété Lake, encircled by white sand dunes. You should try to see the lake in moonlight when students are singing and drinking coconut water. Coconut water is something you will find almost everywhere, especially on all beaches where a young boy is always ready to climb to the top of a coconut tree in exchange for a coin. This lesson in acrobatics is worth the tip and the fresh water of the coconut is delicious.

Coconut water is in fact found inside the nuts themselves. The proper milk is obtained by squeezing out the juice of grated coconuts.

On the other side of the airport is another beach straight out of a dream, deserted and forgotten by the world, Arembepe. The silence is pierced only by the sound of the surf and the whistling of the wind in the coconut palms. This wide expanse of deep blue ocean, white sand and green coconut trees as far as the eye can see is the perfect landscape in which to flee on foot from contemporary civilization.

Salvador, the first capital of Brazil
built on the Bay of All Saints.
Left : The Church of Conceiçao da
Praia brought from Portugal stone
by stone and then assembled on
the site where it now stands.
The chapel of Monte Serrat.
The old cannons at the entrance to
the Bay of All Saints.
Right: The Church and the Solar do
Unhao contrasting with the buildings
of the upper city of Salvador.
Following pages: The ritual of the
washing of the Church of Our Lord
Bonfim: Bahianas in ceremonial
dress, covered with necklaces and
carrying vases of flowers on their
heads with elegance and grace.

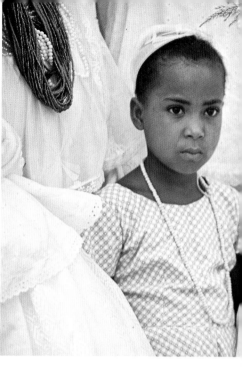

Rich Baroque decoration in
Salvador's churches and
ancient monasteries.
Left from top to bottom: The ceiling
of the Sacristy of the Carmelites.
Detail from the Church of São
Francisco de Assis : the "talha,"
woodwork covered with gold leaf.
The Sacristy of the Carmelites with
furniture made of rosewood.
Right: The center of Salvador
with its palm trees and many
churches which have inspired a
song: "Bahia has 365 churches...".

THE NORTHEAST

In Northeast Brazil, African drums can be heard next to baroque architecture and coconut palms towering over the beaches of white sand bend in the breeze like the coconut trees on the islands of the south seas. The odor of cooking, the melodious intonation of the inhabitants and the myths about the ocean's magic qualities are part of the heritage of the people living in the Northeast. Fishermen, cowboys, farmers and technicians are now involved in solving the eternal problems of this semi-arid region which was only recently penetrated by technological progress. Many of the people live on the coast where rainfall is abundant and sugar cane, bananas, tobacco, coconuts and corn can be grown. The big cities of the region are found along the coast, separated by seemingly endless stretches of fabulous beaches studded with palm trees and fishing villages.

Recife, capital of the State of Pernambuco, is as large as Salvador. Its most famous beach is Noa Viagem. North of Recife is Joao Pessoa, the capital of Paraiba noted for having the Northeast's most modern hotel built on the beautiful beach of Tambau and for the state's gastronomic delight, crab stew. North of Paraiba is the State of Rio Grande do Norte with its salt lagoons and scattered villages of lobster fishermen. The beaches continue northward across the State of Ceara to the State of Maranhao with its charming capital, Saoluis where the architecture is mainly colonial.

Inland, where it is drier, cotton is the most important crop, supplying the raw material for the textile mills of Pernambuco. In the interior of the Northeast, the weather is characterized by a long dry season. In this region, known as the sertao, the temperature generally remains above 75° F; rainfall is irregular with periodic cycles of droughts and floods. The rain, which falls between December and April, is not easily absorbed by the parched earth, and rivers become torrents for short periods of time, flooding the croplands. There is no rain between May and December. In the years in which there is rain, food is plentiful and varied; but in years of drought when the African winds are hot and dry, the earth is scorched and the consequences tragic.

The irrigation projects which are underway and the isolated factories which have been built form part of a concerted effort to relieve the plight of the population in this problem region. Attracting industry to the region is difficult because of the many advantages which are to be found in the South but Northeastern cities are beginning to develop, although slowly compared with cities in other areas of Brazil.

Recife is generally the first stop for tourists arriving in Brazil from North and Central America. This first point of contact lends itself to many dreams. The coconut trees around the airport immediately provide a key to the landscape. The highway from the airport to the city follows the beach of Boa Viagem with a striking view of the Atlantic; the sight is so fabulous that you long to stop and remain forever enwrapped in the enchanting color of the ocean.

Recife, with a population of over a million, is the third port of Brazil, a business, economic and cultural center and one of the largest cities close to the Equator. The city has one of the most rapid rates of industrial growth in Brazil: hundreds of factories have surged out of the earth in a few years in the Paulista and Cabo industrial zones.

Built on peninsulas and islands and cut by two large rivers, the Beberibe and the Capibaribe, Recife owes its typical character to its many bridges. Transformed by progress, the old city is gradually disappearing but the many historical monuments preserved endow Recife with a special atmosphere resulting from a mixture of modern building and baroque churches.

Recife was originally the port of the neighboring town of Olinda, the first capital of the captaincy of Pernambuco. Its name comes from a barrier of coral reefs (*recifes* in Portuguese) protecting the port and extending as far as the beaches in the southern part of the city. The Dutch invasion in the 17th century changed the roles of these two towns: Recife was renamed Mauricéia after the Dutch governor Mauricio de Nassau and became the capital of the Dutch during their period of occupation. Recife has remained the capital of the state of Pernambuco since the Dutch were expelled.

The two decisive battles in which the Dutch were defeated after their 30-year occupation of the Northeast were fought in the Guararapes Hills near Recife in 1648 and 1649. A great 18th century primitive mural of the battle of Guararapes in the church of the Conceição dos Militares shows hundreds of well-dressed Dutch soldiers wearing buckled shoes and breeches fighting the barefoot Brazilians formed into three batallions, white men, Indians and blacks, each led by their leader. Various scenes of the battle are depicted in a picturesque and primitive style. The facade of the historic church of Nossa Senhora das Prazeres, a few miles south of Recife on the very site of the battle, rises among the coconut trees.

The Capela Dourada (Golden Chapel) built by Franciscan monks is the finest of the many churches in Recife, and contains paintings of the eminent figures in the Franciscan Order including Saint Louis, King of France, who was a Franciscan tertiary. Its golden carved altars are a dazzling sight.

The churches of Nossa Senhora do Carmo, Santo Antonio and Nossa Senhora de Concepçao are filled with fine pieces of baroque art. But the most striking church is undoubtedly São Pedro dos Clérigos. It was originally to have been covered with gold like the church of São Francisco de Assis in Salvador but a lack of money prevented this; but today we can still admire the richly carved wood decorations of the altars, ceilings, retables and doors.

The Patío de São Pedro, the square in front of the church of São Pedro dos Clérigos, is an excellent shopping center for handcrafts reflecting the folklore of the region. Small clay statuettes of popular figures working at various skills are a regional speciality created by an old craftsman from the town of Caruaru, Mestre Vitalino, whose many followers keep this local tradition alive.

Caruaru, 80 miles west of Recife, is famous for its big market which is held every Wednesday and Saturday and is considered to be one of the best and cheapest in Brazil where all regional handcraft wares can be found. Tourists looking for typical souvenirs will find everything they desire from all kinds of exotic birds to books of popular poetry hung like laundry on clotheslines and fittingly referred to as *literatura de cordel* (small-cord literature).

A few miles from Recife facing the ocean is a hill so lovely that the Portuguese surveyor sent by Captain Duarte Coelho to find a site on which to build a town exclaimed "O linda" (Oh, the beautiful one), and the second town founded in Brazil was thus named Olinda. Looking at the ocean on one side and Recife on the other from the top of the hill in front of the Cathedral is a thrilling sight. Olinda was a prosperous center for a century and its inhabitants were considered to live in more luxury than did the inhabitants of Lisbon, But it lost its importance after the Dutch invasion in the 17th century when Recife became the capital of the state of Pernambuco.

Olinda is today a small, quiet and poetic city with fine old houses, latticed balconies from which one can see without being seen and 16th and 17th century churches, the prettiest of which, São Francisco de Assis, has a stone cross in front of it and is flanked by a cloister as are all Franciscan monasteries.

If you decide to walk through Olinda, take your time. Enjoy the quiet of this old city and listen to the singing, chanting sound of the wind in the coconut trees. You will eventually reach one of the beaches at the foot of the city were you can take a swim and lunch in a typical restaurant.

As in Recife you can treat yourself to fish and seafood including stuffed *casquinhas de siri,* crabs opened with a stick (the local variety, the *guaiamum,* is succulent) and lobster caught the same day which is less expensive than an ordinary steak.

Fruit abounds in this region and should please all tastes: banana, guava and pineapple as well as *caju, tamarindo, genipapo, maracujá, jambo, carambola, graviola, sapoti, mangaba* and *cajá.* Their very names evoke the light, color and exuberance of the Northeast. Two things not to miss in Recife are the exotic flavors of ice cream and the excellent fruit juice made of fresh fruit especially for you.

The road north along the coast from Recife follows a succession of beaches with white sand stretching endlessy along the blue ocean fringed with coconut trees. The history of Brazil emerges at every stop. The first church in the colony was built in the town of Igaraçu in 1535; and one of its original doors can still be seen. Sugar cane has been grown since the 18th century on the Amparo farm on the island of Itamaraco, an idyllic place with fine beaches, an old Dutch fort and charming villages. In Goiana the restaurants breed their own lobsters and guaiamums. All of these stops on the road from Recife to João pessoa, capital of the state of Paraiba, are colorful and enjoyable.

João Pessoa attracts tourists because of its peaceful atmosphere and location near magnificent beaches as well as its historical colonial collections. One of the most magnificent baroque facades is that of the church of São Francisco; a fort built out into the ocean on Tambaú beach is now an ultramodern hotel; and 12 miles along the coast is the port of Cabedelo, a center for the whaling industry, where you can buy whalebones which will intrigue your friends back home.

The most extreme eastern point of the Northeast is Natal, where Mermoz the French pilot, landed after making the first non-stop flight across the South Atlantic Ocean from Dakar in 1930. Natal was also used as an important stop for ships carrying allied troops to Africa during the second world war. The strategic importance of this place did not escape the attention of the Portuguese who built a fort, the Forte dos Reis Magos, there in the 16th century. One of the best preserved forts in Brazil, it stands out alone against the horizon on a stretch of fine beach.

Running from Natal northwest, one beautiful beach leads to another beautiful beach under a blinding sun. The coconut palms gradually give way to *carnaúbas,* majectic palms whose wax, pouring out of the leaves, can be used for the same purpose as beeswax; and the *babaçus,* palm trees whose nut yields a highly prized wax. We have now reached the state of Ceará and its capital, Fortaleza, which is *par excellence* the home of the *jangadas,* a raft with a sail.

From Bahia to Maranhão the jangadas with their triangular sails endow the Brazilian coast with an incomparable sight which can best be admired at Fortaleza. The ideal way to do this is to spend an afternoon on the beach of Iracema and watch the return of the jangadas at the end of the day.

There are two types of jangada, an invention of the fishermen of Ceara, the traditional sturdy jangada with 6 or 7 beams of light wood simply held together by wooden pegs and never by nails; and the modern jangada, a flat boat painted with bright colors and equipped with a sail and typical accessories of the traditional jangada. The latter include a bench and posts for tying gear; two baskets, a large one for the fish caught and a small one for the bait used; a barrel of fresh water and a container of food; a large, round wooden shovel used for watering down the sail so that it is more resistant to the wind; the *tauassu* or stone used as an anchor and the *fateixa,* another stone used to weight down fishing nets; the *covo,* a net used to capture the fish; a stick to kill the fish; and a long knife used to cut the fish.

The jangada owes its beauty to its triangular sail, fastened to a single mast 20 ft. high and held in position from either side by the boom. The sail is furled around the mast when the jangada is beached; but one the craft is in the sea again, the sail is loosened and seems to float by itself over this flat craft.

The jangadeiro is a simple man who has become sage from contact with the sky, sea and elements. He needs a great deal of courage to spend nights far from the coasts in the company of only a small lantern used signal his presence to other boats. The stars, coconut palms and church belfries are his landmarks in finding the fishing banks and he keeps their exact positions to himself. Jangadeiros have learned to read the grandiose book of nature and under their rough exterior have a sensitive and passionate soul prepared for contemplation when the sunset, firing the heavens, reflects the mysterious bewitching beauty of the Northeast.

Contemplative, the jangadeiro is also a fighter. He exhibits this side of his nature during the annual jangada regatta at Fortaleza. The sea is then covered with sails on the classical triangular course. The first three to reach the beach are entitled to a place on the stand but all competitors receive a prize.

Left: Perched on a hill, Olinda, the first capital of the State of Pernambuco, and, in the background, Recife, a modern city with a population of more than 1,000,000.
Below: Recife, one of the few large cities near the Equator, is located at the junction of the Bereribe and Capibaribe Rivers. Its many bridges give it a typical character and make it a unique tourist spot.

A profusion of fruit, vegetables, coconuts and lobster in restaurants in Recife and Olinda ; the fish and shellfish are delicious and the musical names of the fruit evoke the light, color and exuberance of the Northeast.
Following pages: Jangadas at dawn on a beach at Fortaleza. Traditionally made without nails, primitive and consisting of six or seven light wooden beams, these boats are held together by wooden pegs.

*Left: A young fisherman ; a veteran who knows all the secrets of the ocean ; and a skilled jangadeiro. These simple men have become wise from contact with the sky, the open sea and the elements.
Following pages: The immense salt works at Macau and Areia Branca (White Sands) in Rio Grande do Norte.*

THE AMAZON

The Amazon River, which is the largest in the world has a volume of water equal to 11 times the volume of water in the Mississippi River. It has numerous tributaries which drain the northern region of Brazil. Amazonia, consisting mainly of forest, forms more than 56% of Brazil's national area but only 7% of its total population. Most of the inhabitants of Amazonia live in and around a few cities including Manaus, which is a thousand miles from the ocean, and Belem situated on the Equator, which is a port a few miles from the sea. The jungle is the largest in the world with more flora and fauna—animals, birds, fish, flowers, insects, plants, serpents and trees—than any other jungle in the world. In the 1960's, the government undertook to develop this immense region. Highways are being pushed through the jungle; farms and ranches are being established along these roads; hydro-electric plants are being built; and companies have been formed to exploit the mineral resources of the region— manganese, iron, gold and diamonds.

Unlike most of the great rivers in the world, the Amazon was not discovered through its mouth but rather through the interior of the country. Its estuary, seen from the sea, branches out into hundreds of arms and the first navigators exploring the coast of South America did not realize that they had found the outlet of the biggest river system in the world.

The glory of discovering the Amazon River goes to the Spanish explorer Francisco de Orellana, a companion of Pizzaro during the conquest of Peru. Crossing the Andes and penetrating into the forest on the other side of the mountains, he first reached the Coca River which he descended as far as Napo. In February 1542 he reached the Amazon River at a point 2,135 miles from its mouth. Continuing his voyage, Orellana descended the river to the ocean. From there he went to the West Indies and returned to Spain, claiming to have discovered the longest river in the world.

The expedition was attacked at a place called Nhamunda by Indians whose hairless appearance made the Spanish believe that they were women. The Spanish referred to them as ''Amazons'', the name in Greek mythology for the dangerous female warriors descended from Ares, the terrible god of war, and the nymph Harmony.

The etymology of the word ''amazon'' has been much discussed. Some interpret it as being a = without + mazos = breast as the amazons had lost their right breast in order to use the arc more skillfully. According to another interpretation, the first letter is an augmentative and ''amazon'' consequently means ''a woman with powerful or many breasts''. These creatures would, therefore, be like clouds abundantly shedding water with which the earth is nourished. Nonetheless, it is quite remarkable that in a country like Brazil where geographical names with Indian origins, all of which begin or end with *ita, uba, una, guaçu,* etc., are predominant, the longest river was given a Greek name by the Spaniards.

The size, volume of water—12 times that of the Mississippi—and number of tributaries has no equal in the world. The river is almost 4,000 miles long, more than the distance in a straight line between Paris and New York; it runs for just over 2,000 miles in Brazil, a distance greater than the width of the Atlantic between Natal and Dakar; its average flow is 120,000 m³ a second, which means that it could increase, for example, the water level of Lake Geneva by 3.3 ft. within 81 minutes. Some of its tributaries including the Nadeira, the Purus, the Japura and the Negro, are longer than the Danube, the Ganges, the Zambezi, the Colorado or the Columbia.

This gigantic force of nature floods its banks every year, covering thousands of square miles regularly. The extent of the floods depends on the amount of rainfall and melted snow from the Andes. The water builds up for six months and gradually diminishes in the following six months. Houses are always built on poles along the river and floating stables are quite common.

Considering the proximity of the Equator, there is practically no difference between the seasons. The year can be divided into two periods, winter when it is cool and rainy, and summer when it is warm and dry.

At the mouth of the enormous Amazon River is Belem, whose tree-lined avenues form pleasant and welcoming arches of green vegetation protecting strollers against the heat. Tourists not accustomed to the equatorial climate will be comfortable as are the local kids looking for unripened fruit.

Belem was founded in 1616 by Francisco Caldeira de Castelo Branco, the governor of Grão-Pará. Built, defended and enlarged by the Portuguese, the city has strong traces of Portuguese influence, especially in the old sections, along with modern skyscrapers. As in Lisbon, the facades of many houses are covered with tiles. The most beautiful building, containing the Historical Monuments Agency, seems to have been transported straight from the capital of Portugal.

Tradition has it that it rains in Belem every day at the same hour and that the inhabitants accordingly make their rendez-vous and appointments before or after the rain. This may have been true formerly but today the weather must be changing as the sun may well shine for two days in a row and then on the third it may rain in torrents all day.

Belem today is a big port with a population of more than 700,000. The conventional sightseeing circuit neglects the modern port but not the old dock-side Ver-O-Peso (See-the-weight) Market, named, according to some, after the large scales on which the fish landed nearby were weighed or, according to others, after the inspectors of the Portuguese Royal Treasury who controlled the weight of merchandise and detected fraud.

This colorful market with its fruit, regional handcrafts and boats carrying local products is filled with animation. The ocean tide regulates the activity of boats which flounder on the mud until the tide begins to rise again. The best point from which to enjoy this view is the nearby old fort built by the Portuguese. Its old cannons which guarded the entrance to the river are now silent forever and its garden is a peaceful retreat from the bustle of the city.

Belem is well located for studying the Amazon fauna. Although excursions into the jungle provide you with a close view of the lush vegetation, such trips are disappointing in terms of animals. More than one tourist going off into the Amazon jungle in search of a panther has returned disappointed at having seen only insects. The inhabitants of the region smile when they tell you that panthers only attack humans in movies.

The panther is apparently only dangerous when wounded. You will see very few animals in the jungle, quite simply because they can hear you approaching and scatter. Belem does have an excellent zoo at the Goeldi Museum, which is worth the trip. The Paratur Garden, part of the State Tourist Office, contains many birds and small typical animals.

Your curiosity will probably be aroused by a visit to Turtle Paradise where hundred of these reptiles reproduce in turtle ponds. Here you can see their voracious appetite at work and watch them fight savagely over the leaves thrown to them by the attendant. But don't expect to enjoy a plate of this delicacy; unfortunately for gourmets, eating turtle here is now forbidden by law in an attempt to preserve the species.

Few tourists unfortunately think of visiting the church of Murutucum belonging to the Agronomic Institute near Belem. The church is now just a mass of ruins completely covered by the jungle but highly evocative with roots clinging to the columns and branches passing through the windows and curling over the facade. This sight recalls the Yucatan or Angkor Wat transplanted to the banks of the Amazon.

Visiting the Amazon, tourists will certainly not want to idle away their time on the beautiful beaches of Belem, including Mosqueiro, but will want to spend their time on other discoveries. One sight should be seen, however, Marajó Island, especially its eastern part facing the ocean. The Amazon delta cuts in two a plain bigger than California and more than half the size of Texas with vast stretches of inundated areas in which land and water merge their domains. From Belem you can go by boat to Soure, the main town on the island, or take a small plane to one of the large cattle ranches.

The cowboys on Marajó wear large colored capes made of wool or nylon as protection against frequent cloudbursts and ride horses or buffaloes. The latter appeared on the island following the wreck off the coast of a French boat carrying cattle from Indochina to French Guiana. The buffaloes which managed to reach land soon reproduced. Endowed with a Herculean force, they are better adapted than horses to flooded land, moving their hoofs through the mud without removing them from the soft wet earth.

Nothing is more beautiful on Marajó than the flight of birds in the driest months, from July to September. Flocking together at water holes, they take off by the hundreds all at once. At the approach of an airplane, white herons and all-red *guarás* form a colorful, undulating mass. Fill your eyes with this sight unique in the world as the *guarás* of Florida have been exterminated and the last refuge of this typically equatorial bird is in the Amazon basin.

Some 1,060 miles from the Atlantic, the fort of São José do Rio Negro was founded by Francisco de Mota Galvao in 1669. As there was a tribe of Indians in the vicinity known as the Manaus tribe, the village built around the fort was given this name; and tradition claims that a Portuguese sergeant, who had become the friend of the Indians, married the daughter of the Indian chief.

The growth of such a city so distant from everything and everyone would have been a long and difficult process without the rubber boom at the end of the 19th century and the discovery of vulcanization, a process treating rubber to give it useful properties including elasticity, strength and stability and making it insensitive to temperature variations. In a few years the world consumption of rubber increased a hundredfold and, as the rubber tree from which latex was obtained existed only in Amazonia, exporters of this product made the city prosperous in a very short space of time. The rubber barons built magnificent palaces at the entrance to which they proudly engraved their initials and the date of their success. Such prosperity, however, did not last long.

The streets of Manaus still contain the reminders of this earlier age of wealth: a house covered with Portuguese tiles; a building influenced by the Italian Renaissance, now the Custom Building; the remains of a Rhine castle, now a brewery; a fountain decorated with bronze angel-fish; and sidewalks with sinuous designs like the movement of the water in a river when boats pass by.

Created in 1967, a free duty zone has given Manaus a second youth. Its trade attracts crowds of buyers from Rio and São Paulo; and the inhabitants of Manaus have taken advantage of their new status to offer for sale all the luxury products of the world at prices much cheaper than in any other Brazilian city. The remnants of the golden period of rubber are gradually disappearing and skyscrapers are slowly taking the place of opulent mansions. One of these vestiges, though, is still extant, the Manaus Opera, symbol of its past glory.

If we remember that the jungle is not far away, the interior of the Manaus Opera seems to be a magic vision. Very well conserved, it immediately conjures up the voice of the great Caruso singing ``Pagliacci'' there or the ethereal figure of Anna Pavlova dancing ``Swan Lake'', fabulous images of a period during which opera and ballet companies came directly to Manaus without stopping in Rio de Janeiro.

This luxury suddenly ended in 1912 when plantations in Malaysia began to produce rubber at cheaper cost. One anecdote illustrates the unexpected aspect of this change. Construction of the opera house had not yet been completed; the boat carrying Carrara marble from Italy to be used for the columns in the lobby sank and the funds to buy new marble could not be raised. This marked the end of a period: the present columns made of painted plaster support the ceiling from which hang Venitian crystal chandeliers.

A visit to the Indian Museum in Manaus, which has the largest collection of indigenous objects in the area, is a fascinating experience. Women will admire the beautiful head-dresses made of toucan feathers and men will envy the ring ``used to catch a fiancée'', a kind of women tube which cannot be removed once slipped onto a finger. The collection, lovingly and patiently collected by a Salesian missionary, provides an idea of the customs of the Indians. The visit is especially interesting since the tribes living in the jungle are difficult to visit; in fact, to do so, you must have special permission from the government's Department for the Protection of the Indians. The museum also sells authentic Indian crafts.

The symbol of the revival of Amazonia, the Hotel Tropical in Manaus is an incredible place to stay. Built a few miles from the city on the Negro River, it covers more ground than any other hotel in the world and has opened the doors of the Amazon to international tourism. The patio around the pool is illuminated at night with lights hidden in the plants and is a setting worthy of a tale from the thousand and one nights.

You must leave Manaus to see the jungle at first hand. Depending on the season, you can either walk along paths in the dry season or float along in a canoe during the rainy season. In both cases your impression will be completely different, which should be enough to justify a second trip to Amazonia in order to experience both. The lush vegetation is, in any event, quite fabulous. The branches of the trees shoot up in search of light, indispensable to their growth, and interlace forming an arch similar to a cathedral vault.

Organized boat tours explore the interior of *igarapés*, branches of the river advancing quite a distance into the jungle; the boats drop anchor from time to time to allow you to catch piranhas with bits of meat used as bait. Fishing for piranhas may give you the chills as the teeth of these fish are as sharp as a saw and with a single bite the piranha can cut off a finger or a piece of flesh. Be very careful handling this fish once you have caught it.

The chirping of birds is a real symphony of sound during the day and the buzzing of insects puts you to sleep at night. You sleep in bamboo huts or on boats. In the morning you can swim in places along the river not frequented by piranhas with the guide dispelling your fears by being the first into the water.

Boat tours include stops at houses of the *caboclos*, indigenous people living along the river. These primitive and courageous people are very gentle and quite philosophical. They will display caiman skins, cut gashes in old rubber trees to show you the sap which oozes out, weave palm leaves to cover the roofs of their houses and paddle out of their houses, squatting at the bow of their dugout canoes. These strong Indians have a knowledge of nature which will surprise travellers. How have they learned to tell the difference between an edible and a poisonous fruit, between a dangerous lake with piranhas and one which is not dangerous although the waters of the two run into each other, or between plants which can and cannot soothe insect bites? They have probably inherited their knowledge from their Indian ancestors.

Like Belem, most cities in Amazonia were founded by the Portuguese who named them after Portuguese towns—Bragança, Santarém, Monte Alegre, Alenquer, Chaves, Obidos, and Almeirim. Of these, Santarém, the third largest town in Brazilian Amazonia, is the most interesting for tourists; it is well serviced by plane, has an ultra-modern hotel and is a center for possible excursions.

At dusk boats line up along the port, ready to leave in all directions. These river ''buses'' run at night as the wind is lighter, the river calmer and the air cooler. Each passenger has his own hammock; the atmosphere created is one of warmth and fraternity for both regular passengers and foreigners. The river is a universe bringing men closer to each other, and all passengers feel that they are members of the same family. The tourist not afraid of sleeping in a hammock should experience this new and quite exciting sensation during the trip.

You should take a bus or a car from Santarém over the wide and straight Santarém-Cuiabá road, one of the north-south highways built by the Brazilian army, to the Transamazonic Highway at Troncamento, a distance of 130 miles. The Transamazônica, narrower than the Santarém-Cuiabá highway, was the first road built through the jungle; it skirts natural obstacles and connects Brazil's furthest eastern and western points.

The land along the Transamazônica has been divided into lots 1,650 ft. wide. Each group of 20 families has its own school attended by white, mulatto and black children, a model of racial integration. The prefabricated houses of these farmers are made of wood and are all similar although each family paints its house the color of its choice.

In the 1960's the Amazon regained some economic strength and a new basis of economic development with the infusion of government and private investment capital through tax incentives. The new wave of pioneers arrived.

A stop in one of their houses is an opportunity to discover the personality of these new pioneers: farmers from southern, central or north-eastern Brazil who will not hear any talk about returning to their former place of residence. One member of a family from São Paulo declared: "We could no longer bear the cold there." Now they sleep in hammocks but admit with a smile: "In the beginning we often fell out of our hammocks but gradually we became accustomed to them. We had to. It would be impossible to sleep in a bed with such heat."

Further south you will come across gold prospectors. This excursion can only be done by hiring a plane. A clearing in the jungle suddenly appears in which the inhabitants, completely isolated from the rest of the world, live. They extract gold as did the first pioneers at Ouro Preto or in California, by digging out the earth, washing it in crude basins and separating the gold from the sand by the process of decantation.

Here men are different, adventurers attracted by the prospect of quick profit although the work is difficult. Most are hired and paid on a per diem basis. The concessionnaires exploiting the land can earn a fortune through the sale of gold but, as they must pay their men whether gold is found or not, they run the risks of the operation. One of them may show you the product of five days of work contained in a glass coffee jar, 4½ lbs. of gold in nuggets as large as grains of sand. He may let you touch the gold but will politely ask you to wash your hands in a wash basin.

During the trip the pilot may add a thrill to the flight by landing in the middle of a road and, after turning around, taking off again. Taxi-planes are used in this part of Brazil much as in other parts of the world we would rent a car. A pilot from São Paulo bought a plane on credit and came to the small town of Itaituba on the Tapajós River to try his luck in Amazonia. He earns his living by supplying gold prospectors and using his craft as a taxi-plane. Asked by a friend if he didn't feel as though he were living at the end of the world, he replied: "No. The people who live in Rio, New York or Paris live at the end of the world. We, here, we are at its beginning."

The port of Belem near the Vero-o-Peso Market is
constantly animated. Boats arrive at high tide, are
stranded at low tide and move out of the port
when the waters of the bay rise again.
Following pages: Marajo cowboys on their buffaloes
crossing flooded fields. They wear woolen or nylon
capes as protection against cloudbursts.

Extracting gold in the middle of Amazonia with primitive means. The earth is dug up and carried to rough wooden basins where the gold is separated from the sand by decantation.

Reminders of the former splendor of Manaus during the gilded rubber era: the Opera House and its multicolored dome, houses covered with ceramics and the old Customs House. Exports of latex brought Manaus a fabulous fortune and the city has preserved many vestiges of its former prosperity and great wealth.

The Manaus Opera House where Enrico Caruso sang and Ana Pavlova danced. At that time, opera and ballet companies came directly from Europe to Manaus. This glorious period ended suddenly in 1912 when plantations in Malaysia began to produce rubber at lower cost than the Brazilian produce.
Bottom left: In the lobby, painted plaster columns and real Venetian crystal chandeliers.

Macaws, guaras, crocodiles, boas, storks and toucans provide a colorful, awesome and fascinating fauna. Trips into the jungle provide a first-hand view of the fantastic vegetation but are disappointing because of an absence of animals: once they hear men, they flee. However, examples of Amazon fauna can be seen in the zoological gardens of Belem and of Manaus.

Top left: Exploiting rubber trees, the latex of which brought a temporary fortune to Amazonia.
Bottom left: The flooded jungle known as "igapo" by the Indians. The trees stretch out toward the sky seeking the light which is indispensable to their existence.
Below: In the jungle, rivers form unexpected curves, changing position during floods and abandoning loops of their bed which are gradually covered with vegetation.

Shipyards on the edge of the river, houses on piles, boats on which you sleep in hammocks: all daily events are centered on the banks of the river. Every year the Amazon floods its banks, covering thousands of sq. miles. The flood cycle is fixed and based on the melting of snow from the Andes and on rainfall: the water rises for six months and then falls during the next six months.

The fishermen of Amazonia are strong men with a profound sense of nature. They are rough and courageous, spontaneously nice and highly philosophical.

useful
information

SURI
NAM   FRENCH GUIANA

UY
ANA

MACAPÁ

Amazonas

SANTARÉM

BELÉM

ANÁUS

SÃO LUÍS

FORTALEZA

TERESINA

NATAL

Xingu

JOÃO PESSOA

RECIFE

Tapajós

Tocantins

MACEIÓ

ARACAJU

Araguaia

SALVADOR

São Francisco

ILHÉUS

BRASÍLIA

CUIABÁ

GOIÂNIA

UBERABA   BELO HORIZONTE

VITÓRIA

Paraná

RIBEIRÃO
PRETO

MPO GRANDE

JUIZ DE FORA

MARÍLIA   RIO DE JANEIRO

ARAGUAY

LONDRINA   SÃO PAULO

CURITIBA

FLORIANÓPOLIS

RUGUAIANA

CAXIAS
DO SUL

ATLANTIC OCEAN

PORTO ALEGRE

URUGUAY

141

I. — THE COUNTRY

Size and/location geographical.

Brazil, the fifth largest country in the world after the Soviet Union, Canada, China and the United States, has an area of 3,286,473 sq. miles. It is bigger than Western Europe, almost as large as the United States (3,615,122 sq. miles) and nearly half the size of South America. Brazil borders on all the other countries in South America except Chile and Ecuador. Brazil has a coastline on the Atlantic Ocean of just over 4,600 miles and extends 2,689 miles from North to South and 2,684 miles from East to West. The northern extremity of the country is cut by the Equator and the southern part by the Tropic of Capricorn which runs through the center of Sao Paulo. The land is still not yet spoiled by pollution; and at any time of the year visitors can find bright sun and pure air so rare elsewhere.

Time

Official Brazilian time, known as "Brasilia Time," is G.M.T. — 3, effective on the coast and throughout most of the country. Only the western part of central Amazonia, including the major cities of Manaus and Santarem, is different with time 4 hours behind G.M.T.

The difference in time between New York and Rio de Janeiro is 2 hours; and between Los Angeles and Rio 5 hours. When it is 12 noon in New York and 9 a.m. in Los Angeles, it is 2 p.m. in Rio.

Geographical regions

Brazil is generally divided into five large geographical regions, according to a number of characteristics including topography, type of vegetation and the administrative areas of its 21 states. The five regions are the North, the Northeast, the Southeast, the South and the Central West.

1. The north

The North is the largest Brazilian region and one of the least populated areas in the world (2 1/2 inhabitants per sq. mile). Accounting for 42% of Brazil's land surface, it has one of the most fascinating landscapes in the world, the Amazon river basin and jungle, source of half the oxygen supply of our planet. Its climate is warm and humid.

The topography is low but not flat; and the rivers of the Amazon basin form countless valleys. In the extreme northern part of this region are moutain ranges separating Brazil from the Guianas and Venezuela. The highest mountain in Brazil is found here, Pico da Neblina (10,046 ft.) on the Venezuela border. The North comprises the states of Acre, Amazonas and Para and the federal territories of Roraima, Rondonia and Amapa.

2. The Northeast

Fertile valleys with coconut palms and sugar-cane plantations alternate with semi-arid stretches of land periodically hit by drought. Almost a quarter of Brazil's population lives in the Northeast, the surface area of which represents only 11.5% of the country. On the coast, the climate is warm but cooled by ocean breezes. The arid interior, or sertão, is often scorchingly hot.

The Northeast consists of the states of Naranhão, Piauí, Ceará, Rio Grande do Norte, Paraiba, Pernambuco and Alagoas.

3. The Southeast

The Southeast region, a transitional area between the Northeast and the South, consists almost entirely of mountains the geological structure of which is high in mineral deposits. Its surface represents one seventh of that of Brazil and its population one third of the total population. The climate of this region is temperate due to its altitude except along the coast between Bahia and Rio de Janeiro where it is hot. This region has five states, Sergipe, Bahia, Espirito Santo, Minas Gerais and Rio de Janeiro. The latter state consists of the territories of the former state of Rio de Janeiro the capital of which was Niteroi and the former Federal District of the city of Rio de Janeiro.

4. The South

The South is the most higly developed part of Brazil. It represents only one tenth of the total area of the country but has one third of Brazil's population. It stretches out almost entirely over a very fertile plateau cascading sharply to the coast but falling gently off toward the interior. Vegetation is quite different from that in other regions of the country as the seasons are well defined and winters can be harsh. In the southern part of this region, the mountains gradually fall away to the famous pampas, rolling grasslands with huge cattle and sheep ranches. The South consists of four states, São Paulo, Paraná, Santo Catarina and Rio Grande do Sul.

5. The Central West

The Central West region is characterized by vast *cerrados,* fields with short, stubby trees. Although it covers 22% of Brazil's area, its population only represents 5% of Brazil's total population. Rio de Janeiro was replaced as the capital of the country by Brasilia in 1960 in a bold attempt to further the development of the immense underdeveloped central and western plateaus. In addition to the Federal District of Brasilia, the region has two states, Goiás and Mato Grosso.

II. — POPULATION

The population of Brazil is now over 120,000,000 inhabitants. Three races have contributed to its growth, the original Indian inhabitants, the Portuguese who discovered the country in 1500 and colonized it, and the Blacks brought from Africa as slaves.

Since the mid-19th century, many Italians, Germans, Poles, Lebanese and Japanese have immigrated, especially to the South.

Most of the inhabitants live along the coast where the races have blended into the most varied range of human types and skin colors. As you go inland, the *caboclo* sunburnt type, the heir to the three races, gradually predominates.

Religion

Most Brazilians (95%) are Catholic and remain faithful to the traditions of the Catholic Church; the Brazilian Constitution was promulgated "in the name of God;" and Christian morality is the basic tenet of family life.

Belfries add a typical note to the landscape of the smallest villages.

However, Catholicism has been mixed to a certain extent with animism and African rites among the poorly educated.

A few Protestants are found throughout the country.

Language

The language of Brazil is Portuguese, spoken more openly and slowly than in Portugal. There are no dialects despite the size of the country although some words have different meanings in different regions.

If you do not speak Portuguese, you can get along fairly well with either English or Spanish. Since Brazilians are sensitive about their language, you should make an effort to learn a few words of Portuguese if you do not speak it fluently.

III. — MEANS OF TRANSPORTATION IN BRAZIL

BETWEEN CITIES

1. Plane

A recent Varig poster proclaimed that "our domestic airlines are for Brazil the equivalent of the Swiss railway for Switzerland." The comparison is not exaggerated: Brazil has a highly developed domestic air service connecting its major cities and operating at varying daily frequencies.

Considering the immense size of Brazil, the plane is the indispensable means of transportation in reaching important places in a short time.

Four private companies share the traffic—Varig, Cruzeiro, Vasp and Transbrasil. The first two have merged and account for almost two thirds of all domestic flights. Almost all planes used are jets with one class.

Some cities are connected by shuttle service, Rio and São Paulo, Rio and Brasilia, Rio and Belo Horizonte, and Belo Horizonte and Brasilia. For the shuttle service, you simply go to the airport, buy a ticket and take the first plane leaving. The four airlines share this service so that, if there is no place on one flight, you can always be assured of finding a seat on the next flight.

2. Buses

All major Brazilian cities (except those in the Amazon) are connected by regular bus service. The service is fast and extremely comfortable; most buses are air-conditioned and some have reclining seats with foot and leg rests. The roads are excellent but bus trips can be long and tiring because of the long distances involved. For example, the 1,067 miles between Rio de Janeiro and Salvador take two days and one night to cover by bus.

If you have the time and the desire to travel economically, buses are the most highly recommended means of transportation.

3. Car

Some car rental companies will rent you a car in one city and allow you to return it in another city against a small charge for the return trip.

Taxis can also be hired for excursions and trips. Be sure to agree on the price in advance.

However, because of the distances involved, hiring a car is only interesting for short trips, such as Rio-São Paulo (250 miles). It is much more economical to use planes or buses for long distances and to rent a car at each stop for local sightseeing.

4. Ship

A number of shipping lines operate regular passenger boat services along the coast, with stops in major cities. This is an interesting way to discover the country although less practical than by bus, the schedules of which are much more frequent and more easily adaptable to personal options.

Special cruises run from Rio to Manaus in the heart of the Amazon region and stop at various ports. The boats are excellent but the stops are sometimes too short. Along with the pleasure of cruising on a fine boat, you will discover the coast and the Amazon River.

5. Air taxi

All of Brazil's large cities have several air taxi com-companies which rent planes carring 3,5 or 7 passengers; some companies even have bigger planes for rent. This is obviously a convenient, rapid means of transportation but one which is not within the price range of most tourists.

In the Amazon, however, the air taxi is a local institution. As long as all passengers share the cost of the flight, it is quite reasonable. Companies in Belem, Santarem and Manaus fly single or twin-engine planes equipped with radio and meeting safety regulations.

These planes are the only means of visiting cattle ranches on Marajo Island as well as gold prospecting sites in the jungle. The cost of such flights may be included in package tours if such excursions are part of the initial trip.

IN CITIES

1. Car rental

In all major Brazilian cities, you can rent a car, often at the airport.

All the cars have been produced domestically. The most popular and least expensive is the Volkswagen Beetle; such cars as the Brasilia, Chevette, Corcel or Dodge are slightly more expensive. Big cars— Maverick, Opala, Galaxie—are very comfortable but cost twice as much to rent.

To rent a car, you must have a passport and an international driver's license and pay the rental charge in advance. Some companies accept credit cards.

Cars can be reserved from one city to another without difficulty. However, reservations made from abroad are not guaranteed, especially during Carnival and in July.

Renting a car is an ideal means of visiting some cities including Rio de Janeiro and Salvador where distances are great; it is also highly recommended for excursions to Ouro Preto and Congonhas do Campo from Belo Horizonte.

2. Taxis

Taxis are inexpensive but difficult to find during rush hours. Fares are indicated on a meter and it is customary to give the driver a tip.

You can also arrange with a taxi driver for a tour of the city for an hourly rate. This is more interesting than renting a car, especially if you only have one day available for sightseeing, as the driver's knowledge will save you a great deal of time.

3. Organized tours

In all cities organized tours on buses or mini-buses with guides is a good way of becoming acquainted with a city, especially if you have little time for visiting tourist sites. It is certainly the ideal way of visiting Brasilia in a few hours. Hotels and travel agencies can provide you with all information on such tours.

IV. — PREPARING YOUR TRIP

The Best time of year
There is no best time of year to visit Brazil. The best months vary from region to region, but there is no period which is really bad. The difference between the seasons of the year is much less well defined than in most of the United States and a trip to Brazil can be made under good conditions at any time of the year.

The weather in various parts of Brazil can be characterized as follows:

In Rio de Janeiro, the weather is hot between November and April and more temperate between May and October. You can go swimming throughout the year in Rio.

In Sao Paulo, the summers are quite comfortable but the winters may be very cold.

In Rio Grande do Sul and Minas Gerais, the winters are colder but the days are fine. The temperature may fall below freezing in Ouro Preto in August.

In Brasilia, at an altitude of 3,960 ft., the weather is never very hot or very cold; the climate of Brasilia is quite healthy.

Salvador and Recife are never cold. It is quite hot there but ocean breezes generally make things bearable. You can go swimming at any time.

In Amazonia the temperature remains between 77° and 81° throughout the year. But the humidity is high and you may initially have some difficulty in adapting to the climate.

Carnival — whether in Rio with its parade of the Samba clubs or in Salvador de Bahia with its festivities in the street — is a tourist attraction which will determine the date of a visit to Brazil for many tourists. Carnival is held on Shrove Tuesday and the three preceding days, seven weeks before Easter.

Baggage
The golden rule for modern travellers in any part of the world is to take only as much baggage as you can carry yourself. This is virtually a necessity if you travel by plane since you only have the right to 66 lbs. in First Class and 44 lbs. in Economy Class.

For a trip to Brazil which may involve different kinds of activities (tourism, social events, sports), we advise that your take two pieces of luggage.

1) a solid, but light, suitcase;

2) a bag no more than about 12 in. long carried over your shoulder and used for multiple purposes: on the plane, as hand baggage (the length mentioned above meets regulations on the size of carry-on baggage); it can easily be placed under your legs without bothering your neighbors and can be used as a foot-rest at night;

on excursions, it can be used to carry cameras, film, bathing suit, towel, books and sweaters;

on overnight trips, it can be used to carry pyjamas, toilet articles and spare clothes, if needed;

at the beach, it can be used to carry towels, sun lotions, books and games.

Two-week trips

Two-week trips

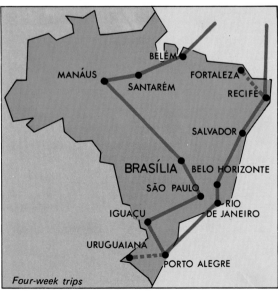

Four-week trips

Things to take with you

Except for temperate zones between May and September, you will probably find Brazil hot and should only take summer clothes with you including:

1. a suit or two dresses for evening wear;
2. two pair of light-weight, comfortable pants or two skirts; shorts can generally be worn anywhere;
3. several shirts;
4. a bathing suit;
5. a soft, washable hat;
6. an easily folded raincoat, taking up little space;
7. one or two light pyjamas;
8. Several pair of light socks;
9. a pair of shoes for the city and a comfortable pair of walking shoes; in Amazonia you should have a pair of tennis shoes which protect your feet and dry quickly. if you get them wet; boots are not needed; and at the beach you can wear sandals;
10. a light sweater for the plane and cool evenings.

In addition, for short trips to Minas Gerais, São Paulo or Rio Grande do Sul between May and September, you should take a heavy dress or pair of pants, one or two winter shirts or blouses, a heavy sweater and woollen socks.

Don't forget to take the following items:

1. sun glasses;
2. plastic bags for wet bathing suits and dirty clothes;
3. any medicine which you use;
4. a camera (be sure that the batteries are still good);
5. enough film for the trip; otherwise, you will find that film is more expensive in Brazil.

You need take no special precautions to protect your film but you should have films developed immediately after your return.

You can easily find in Brazil:

1. anti-mosquito products;
2. current pharmaceutical products;
3. sun lotions;

Documents

All tourists must have a valid passport. Visas are not required for stays of up to 90 days by tourists from American and Western European countries.

Currency

Any amount of foreign currency may be brought into Brazil along with a reasonable amount of Brazilian cruzeiros. U.S. dollars are easy to exchange anywhere in the country.

You should carry most of your money in travellers checks. In case of loss or theft, the travellers checks will be replaced in Brazil by the branch of the bank which issued them. You should note the numbers of your travellers checks on a piece of paper which you should keep separate from your billfold.

You should also have ten or twenty $1 bills with you to be used for tipping or small, last-minute purchases, especially when you go into other South American countries.

Credit cards (American Express, Diner's Club) are widely accepted in hotels, restaurants and stores.

The Brazilian currency unit is the cruzeiro (Cr$) divided into 100 centavos.

Customs

Tourists can enter Brazil with a reasonable amount of personal effects, a camera, a movie camera and a portable tape recorder.

V. HOTELS AND RESTAURANTS

Tourist facilities are developing rapidly in Brazil under the impetus of Embratur, the Brazilian Tourist Office. Modern hotels, especially hotels of the Tropical chain, are being built where previously there were practically no such facilities. The most discriminating tourist can now travel through Brazil under very comfortable, and often luxurious, conditions.

Reservations, prices, tipping

You should make hotel reservations well in advance of your arrival if you plan to be in Brazil when it is crowded. Brazilians travel a great deal throughout their country. During the summer (January, February) and in the winter in July when school is out, the main tourist centers and beaches are very crowded. The same is true of extended weekends. As elsewhere in the world, hotel and restaurant prices are generally more expensive during these periods.

You should remember that it is almost impossible to find hotel rooms in Rio de Janeiro and Salvador during Carnival without reservations.

The cost of a hotel in any given city will depend on its category. In most cases service is included in the bill. Small tips should be given, however, to porters. Breakfast is generally also included in the price of a room.

In restaurants where service is not included, a 10 % tip is usual.

Choosing a hotel

There are too many hotels to provide a complete list here; in addition, new hotels are constantly opening. The best guide to hotels and prices is the Guia Quatro Rodas do Brazil, published annually and containing information on all hotels and restaurants in major cities, classified according to category.

For those planning to reserve hotel rooms in advance, the following information should be useful.

1. Rio de Janeiro

You will never forget the view from a room in a hotel overlooking the Parque do Flamengo, especially if it gives on the Sugar Loaf. It is too far from the beach for a quick swim but the vista is fabulous and the prices are reasonable.

You will also keep an unforgettable souvenir of the view on the ocean from a room in a hotel overlooking Copacabana Beach; to take a swim all you need do is cross the avenue. Here, of course, the prices of hotels are much more expensive. If you really want to profit from the proximity of the beach, you can economize by looking for a room without a view on the beach or finding a hotel in one of the side streets. The more luxurious hotels are found further on, overlooking the sea on Avenida Niemeyer and on Sao Conrado Beach. These hotels are recommended for conventions and for those who have a means of transportation at their disposition.

2. Saõ Paulo, Belo Horizonte and Porto Alegre

All the good hotels are located in the center of these cities.

3. Iguaçu Falls

Several pleasant hotels in the National Park. Only one, the Hotel Cataratas, overlooks the falls. It is generally solidly booked and reservations are a must.

4. Ouro Preto

The small, but comfortable, hotels in old mansions

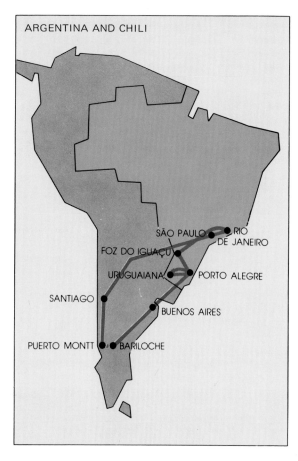

ARGENTINA AND CHILI

SÃO PAULO
RIO DE JANEIRO
FOZ DO IGUAÇU
URUGUAIANA
PORTO ALEGRE
SANTIAGO
BUENOS AIRES
PUERTO MONTT
BARILOCHE

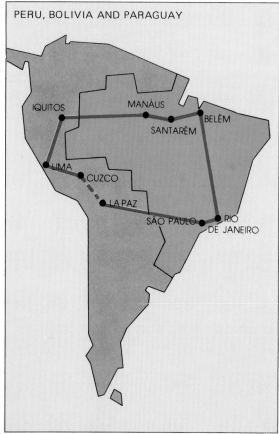

PERU, BOLIVIA AND PARAGUAY

IQUITOS
MANÁUS
BELÉM
SANTARÉM
LIMA
CUZCO
LA PAZ
SÃO PAULO
RIO DE JANEIRO

are highly recommended. Because they have few rooms, reservations should be made in advance. The Grande Hotel is modern and well located.

Congonhas do Campo has a number of modest hotels.

5. Brasilia

The rooms of hotels in the center overlooking the Congress have a beautiful view of the Brazilian capital. Reasonably priced rooms can be found in Brasilia.

The Brasilia Palace Hotel, on the lake not far from the Alvorada Palace, is somewhat distant from the center but very quiet.

6. Salvador

Here you can choose between hotels on the superb beaches but far from the picturesque sections of Salvador, or hotels centrally located and more convenient for visiting the city.

For those planning to stay in Salvador for a while, choosing a hotel along one of the beaches is probably the best arrangement; on the other hand, if you have only one or two days in Salvador, you should choose a centrally located hotel.

7. Recife

Hotels along the Boa Viagem Beach are highly recommended. The center of Recife is not far, which leaves you with the best of all possible worlds, magnificent views on the ocean and easy access to tourist sites.

8. Belem

Hotels in the center of Belem are comfortable. However, since distances are not very great here, we suggest the Selton Hotel outside the city and not far from the airport. The pool and quiet atmosphere will make your stay more enjoyable.

9. Manaus

The Hotel Tropical, outside the city, is a fabulous piece of architecture deserving a visit, even if you do not plan to stay there. At night the patio of the pool is a marvellous sight. The hotel organizes all kinds of excursions including fishing trips and outings to sporting events.

Meals

Meals are generally served as follows:
breakfast: between 7 and 10 a.m.
lunch: between noon and 2 p.m.
dinner: between 7 and 9 p.m.

Breakfast in hotels is generally copious with fruit, ham and cheese in addition to coffee, bread, butter and jam. Its price is almost always included in the price of the room but some hotels add a service charge if breakfast is served in your room.

For lunch you have a wide range of expensive, moderatly priced or inexpensive restaurants in addition to snack bars. Tourists with little time to spare should eat a quick, light lunch; they will consequently be more alert after lunch for sight-seeing and will also have more time for visiting and taking pictures, since everyone else is having lunch. However, in the evening it is very pleasant to take your time over dinner in an open-air restaurant, especially one overlooking the sea. Brazilians remain at table until quite late, drinking light beer or *batida*, the national drink, a cocktail made of local rum and tropical fruit juices.

For those who like wine, Brazil produces good wines which can be ordered in all restaurants.

Choosing a restaurant

The Guia Quatro Rodas do Brasil contains a complete list of restaurants for each city, according to category. For the major cities, they are first indicated by district and then by type of cooking (international, Portuguese, Italian, Chinese, French, Spanish, German, Japanese, Arab, Swiss, seafood, pizza, grilled food, Brazilian specialities).

The guide also indicates by a red mark those restaurants located in a particularly nice setting or having a beautiful view.

VI. — GENERAL INFORMATION

National holidays

National holidays in Brazil are:
— January (New Year) ;
— April 21 (anniversary of the death of Tiradentes, a Brazilian hero) ;
— May 1 (Labor Day) ;
— September 7 (Independence Day) ;
— November 15 (anniversary of the proclamation of the Republic) ;
— December 25 (Christmas).
Many states and cities have their own local holidays.

Electric current

The electric current in Brazil is generally 110 volts, 60 cycles.
You should take a plug adaptor for electrical shavers and other appliances; electric plugs are of the kind found in France, not in the United States.

Shopping and souvenirs

Stores are generally open daily Monday to Friday from 8:30 a.m. to 6:30 p.m.; they are closed Saturday afternoon and Sunday.

In all cities shops selling souvenirs and folk crafts offer an excellent selection of articles made of wood, leather, stones, butterfly wings, cloth, pottery and soapstone. Items are available for all tastes and at all prices, but you should be careful about excess weight on the flight back home.

Among the more popular souvenirs are:
— semi-precious stones:
topaz,
tourmaline,
 aqua-marine
amethyst;
— ashtrays and paper weights made of stone;
— coffee spoons with inlaid small stones;
— cheese dishes made of wood;
— pictures made of butterfly wings;
— rugs or puffs made of cowhide;
— stuffed exotic animals;
— necklaces made of small fruit or grains;
— belts and bracelets made of wood;
— silver ornaments;
— cotton hammocks;
— nylon hammocks;
— tortoise-shell objects;
— pottery.

Communications abroad

International telephone calls can be made and telex messages sent from most parts of Brazil to all the cities in the world via the Intelsat system.

Telephone calls to the United States and Europe can be made automatically from most large cities. International calls made from cities not yet connected to the Intelsat systems must pass through an operator.

Calls can be made from your hotel or from public booths installed by Embratel, the Brazilian telephone company.

Telex messages can also be sent from these booths.

Domestic communications

All large Brazilian cities are connected by an automatic trunk dialing system called DDD. Any city not connected to this system can be obtained by calling the operator.

For local calls, all cities are equipped with many public telephone booths. These large orange shells known as *orelhões* (big ears) are easy to find. Tokens *(ficha de telefone* in Portuguese), bought from bars, cafes and news vendors, are used in these phone booths instead of coins.

Suggestions for sight-seeing trips in Brazil

Travellers with one, two, three or four weeks at their disposition have a number of possibilities available for seeing Brazil. Below are suggestions for possible circuits leaving from Rio de Janeiro. The more time, the better, of course; but it is not always possible to combine the requirements of business with the pleasures of travel. If, on the other hand, you are a leisurely tourist in Brazil, you will never have a dull moment!

Trips of less than one week

a) Busy travellers, businessmen or tourists in transit with no more than 24 or 48 hours in Brazil at their disposition should have no hesitation about what to do; they should stay in Rio, visiting the city and enjoying it as much as possible.

b) Those staying three days will be able to take a one-day round-trip excursion to Brasilia to visit the new Capital.

c) Those with between 4 and 7 days have a choice between the following trips to which they should devote at least two days each:
— Salvador de Bahia;
— Belo Horizonte (for visits to Ouro Preto and Congonhas);
— Iguacu Falls.

Two-week trips

We can suggest two different itineraries, each with 8 stops.
a) Along the coast.

b) In the interior of the country.

Three or four-week trips

We suggest an itinerary combining the coastal and interior circuits. Consisting of 11 stops, it can be covered in three or four weeks.
Those with a little more time will also be able to include: a round-trip from Porto Alegre to Uruguaiana for a visit to the pampa; a round-trip from Recife to Fortaleza for a visit to the Northeast.

Trips including other South American countries

Tourists with a month or more may wish to visit other South American countries. We suggest two possibilities, one including trips to Argentina and Chile, and the other including trips to Peru, Bolivia and Paraguay.
In addition to stops on the three-week trip to Brazil, this itinerary includes:
Peru:
— Iquitos, Peru, in the upper Amazon;
— Lima, capital of Peru;
Bolivia:
— Cuzco and an excursion to Machu-Pichu;
— train trip from Cuzco to Puno and across Lake Titicaca by boat La Paz, capital of Bolivia;
Paraguay:
— Asuncion, capital of Paraguay.

Photographs were taken by Carlos de Sá Moreira,
except those on pages 5, 16, 18, 24, 25, 26, 27,
which were taken by Bernard Hermann.

BRAZIL
Fifth edition: October 1986
Publisher's number: 362
Printed in Singapore
by Tien Wah Press